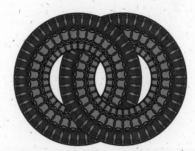

The Waiting Room Reader

VOLUME II

Words to Keep You Company

The Waiting Room Reader

VOLUME II

Words to Keep You Company

Rachel Hadas

Guest Editor

CavanKerry ◈ Press LTD.

CavanKerry Press Ltd.
Fort Lee, New Jersey
www.cavankerrypress.org

Library of Congress Cataloging-in-Publication Data

The waiting room reader II : words to keep you company
/ guest editor, Rachel Hadas. -- 1st ed.
p. cm.
ISBN 978-1-933880-34-1 (alk. paper) --
ISBN 1-933880-34-1
(alk. paper)
1. American poetry--21st century. I. Hadas, Rachel.

PS617.W353 2013
811'.608--dc23

2012024564

Cover design by Gregory Smith, based on a
painting by Gray Jacobik
First Edition 2013,
Printed in the United States of America

LaurelBooks are fine collections of poetry and prose
that explore the many poignant issues associated with
confronting serious physical and/or psychological illness.
The Waiting Room Reader series is an extension of the
LaurelBooks imprint.

CavanKerry is grateful to the Arnold P. Gold Foundation
for Humanism in Medicine for joining us in sponsoring
this imprint. Together with the Gold Foundation,
CavanKerry's outreach efforts bring complimentary
books and readings to the medical community at major
hospitals across the United States.

CavanKerry Press is grateful for the support it receives
from the New Jersey State Council on the Arts

Gratitudes

CavanKerry offers heartfelt thanks to the following
friends whose generosity makes
The Waiting Room Reader II possible:

Co-sponsors:
The Arnold P. Gold Foundation for Humanism in Medicine
Deborah and Brian Henry

Benefactors:
Judith and John Hannan
Susan and John Jackson
Eddie Kaye Thomas
(le) poisson rouge music & arts club

Fundraising Committee:
Carol Snyder, CavanKerry Press Board President: Chair
Robert Gurmankin   Judith Hannan   Deborah Henry
Susan Jackson

Coordinator:
Josh Kashinsky

Designer:
Greg Smith

Cover Artist:
Poet/painter Gray Jacobik, on whose painting
the cover is based

Writers:
The scores of poets and prose writers who offered their
work to this book

Guest Editor:

Rachel Hadas for her commitment to and artistic vision
for *The Waiting Room Reader II*

Contents

Editor's Note

When I think of people in waiting rooms, including myself, I picture us rifling restlessly through battered magazines. No doubt the image is out of date; these days, we're more likely to be texting or talking on cell phones or playing solitaire on some tiny device. No matter: the nervous impatience of the mood in that room doesn't change. The very situation of waiting, of enduring a period of time of unknown duration in a special place reserved for just such endurance, sends most of us on a skittish quest for news from outside the waiting room. If word about our test results or our loved one's condition isn't immediately available (and if it were, why would we be there?), we turn to speedier bulletins to distract ourselves. Current events, celebrity gossip, auto racing, trout fishing—take your pick, and I haven't even mentioned the TV that's likely to be on. All the while, of course, our minds are busily engaged in a dance of avoidance and dread. It's hard to focus on anything.

There's another sort of waiting as well. This kind, which takes place in nursing homes, involves patience rather than fear. But what both flavors of waiting demand, in their respective styles, is steadfastness—the ability to stick with the situation. In circumstances where we can do little but just be there, it helps to pay attention to something. Paying attention to one particular thing rather than flipping pages or scrolling text prevents us from being distracted and thus, paradoxically, can successfully distract us—can move our minds, if only briefly, from the claustrophobic space and the repetitive scenarios in which we may feel trapped.

This book, the second in the *Waiting Room Reader* series, grows from the belief of its visionary originators, Joan Cusack Handler, publisher of CavanKerry Press, and Sandra O. Gold, president of The Arnold P. Gold Foundation for Humanism in Medicine, that one good thing to be able to pay attention to in waiting rooms is poetry. This is a belief that I, as guest editor of this volume, emphatically share. Poems with staying power are always themselves acts of attentiveness, and reading any good poem both demands and rewards attention. The job, then, is to make sure poems can be found in waiting rooms, where they will always be needed. In soliciting work for this book, a book which is intended to find its way into the hands of many people in many waiting rooms, I wasn't after uplift or consolation. I sought poems whose focused engagement might hook the reader, who, once drawn in, might just lose herself in the poem.

I didn't want narratives (which you get in newspapers and magazines) or conversations (which you get in cell phone or texting exchanges); I wanted nouns. I found myself choosing poems that memorably presented things: beets, a scar, a sweater, a bird's nest, a dog. But of course poems function like verbs too. All the works in this collection (primarily poems but also a handful of short prose pieces) enact longing and memory; they recall, they evoke, they praise. The writing of just about every piece in this book turns out to have been an act of reclamation, an evocation of some lost original, which isn't so lost after all. The opening poem, Daniel Brown's tiny "So Large," connects childhood to adulthood; the world's scale changes, but it's the same big sky. Jessica Greenbaum's poem "Gratitude's Anniversary," which closes the collection, performs a similar gesture of folding the past into the present. Greenbaum's title would work well for this anthology as a whole; although she may not have intended this meaning, one thing I take away from "Gratitude's Anniversary" is that even if we're not able to feel grateful for a particular day—say, a day spent in the waiting room—nevertheless every day is the anniversary of a day we can bless.

The sixty-three poems and fourteen prose pieces gathered here touch upon themes poets have always visited: memory, family, love, loss, nature. Voices and styles naturally and delightfully vary; some pieces are chiseled and succinct, others loose and rhapsodic. But all, in addition to being accomplished, share the generosity and intensity of their attention to a particular piece of experience. To read through the many submissions and choose the best writers, and then from their work to choose no more than one poem or prose piece per writer (a rule I made for myself), and then to arrange the resulting pile into something like an arc, something like a story, and something like a conversation, was a very pleasurable challenge. It was a task I undertook in the summer and fall of 2011 at a time late in my husband's life when I myself was putting in many hours in ERs and ambulances and waiting rooms. All the more, then, was I reminded of the eloquence of poetry in such places.

Some of the writers whose work is gathered here are the authors of many books and the winners of many awards; others are closer to the beginnings of their careers. A few are students in or recent graduates of the MFA program at Rutgers–Newark, where I teach, and are therefore at the start of their careers as published writers; I take particular pride in being able to include their fine work. It is my ardent hope that the most restless or distracted rifler through these pages may happen upon a poem, a stanza, a line, or an image that will absorb her, remind her, focus her, make her laugh—whatever she needs at that moment. After all, that's how poetry works.

I am most grateful to Joanne Chin, my very able assistant (and a fiction writer in the Rutgers MFA program whose work is included here), without whose help this volume could never have been assembled so swiftly or so well. And my tremendous gratitude goes out to Joan Cusack Handler of CavanKerry Press, whose vision of *The Waiting Room Reader* has become a reality with the help of the generous assistance of the Liana Foundation and The Arnold P. Gold Foundation for Humanism in Medicine. Along with these words, all of us send our thoughts to people in waiting rooms everywhere.

Rachel Hadas
New York City, March 2012

In memory of my husband George Edwards (1943-2011)

And for people in waiting rooms everywhere:
may this book touch you.

The Waiting Room Reader

VOLUME II

Words to Keep You Company

So Large

Big world when I was very young.
The shopping aisles a mile long . . .
Our lawn, though anything but wide,
Unfolding like a countryside . . .
The sky! So large and far away . . .
Exactly as it is today.

Daniel Brown

Prepositional

Above our heads, a ceiling.

Across the ceiling, a wide sky.

Around the house, birdsong.

Between you and me, a table.

On the table, bread and salt.

Behind us, breadcrumbs

Against a wandering forest.

Before this, a long wandering.

Beneath us, a rich meadow.

Or beneath us, quicksand.

Since then meadows, quicksand.

In you, something, as of a raft.

In me, something like weather.

Beyond, a back-lit bank of clouds.

Lorna Knowles Blake

As If There Were Only One

In the morning God pulled me onto the porch,
A rain-washed gray and brilliant shore.

I sat in my orange pajamas and waited.
God said, "Look at the tree." And I did.

Its leaves were newly yellow and green,
slick and bright, and so alive it hurt

to take the colors in. My pupils grew
hungry and wide against my will.

God said, "Listen to the tree."
And I did. It said, "Live!"

And it opened itself wider, not with desire,
but the way I imagine a surgeon spreads

the ribs of a patient in distress and rubs
her paralyzed heart, only this tree parted

its own limbs toward the sky—I was the light in that sky.
I reached in to the thick sweet core

and I lifted it to my mouth and held it there
for a long time until I tasted the word

tree (because I had forgotten its name).
Then I said my own name twice softly.

Augustine said, *God loves each of us as if
there were only one of us,* but I hadn't believed him.

And God put me down on the steps with my coffee
and my cigarettes. And, although I still

could not eat nor sleep, that evening
and that morning were my first day back.

Martha Serpas

The Two Cedars

From a small, wingback chair
two cedar trees are visible.
The subdivision beyond
has been built up
over two years,
and the streetlights for it
have yet to light night's entrance.
One of the cedars is dead.
The other one, assumedly planted
        at the same time,
appears to be hearty, and even,
to some degree, stately.
They have been companionable,
and have known together
some distance of time.
The wind affects both.
The rain, only one.

Benjamin K. Rogers

Climbing a Fallen Tree

I am bedeviled by many fears, but strangely, and somewhat ironically, a fear of heights is not, has never been, one of them. I remember being small, five or six, gamely traversing the tarred pole, former trunk of another tree, that was laid between two concrete stepped piles that looked like ossified dinosaur dung. Look, Ma, I can do it! I wanted to shout as I learned my balance on that pole and crossed and re-crossed those piles in a throwaway kids park in the Ironbound one summer evening in early 1970-something. But Ma, sitting on a bench by the fence, was looking down into her hands, which were upturned on her lap as if she were pondering two very different lifelines, or supplicating God in Heaven or god of the streetlight.

At five or six, it's hard to tell which. And it hardly matters.

Just as it hardly matters that now, 35 plus years on, I can layer the story a bit and say the glimmer of the streetlight, fastened above us on another embalmed tree trunk, mirrored the glimmer at the corners of her eyes: She was in a bad marriage. She was in her mid-20s and her life was not in her hands. She was disappointed. But I was disappointed too. I had just crossed a pole raised as high off the ground as I was tall, a distance doubled by my standing barefoot on that creosote pole. But she had not seen it. No one had seen it.

Granted, being a handful of feet in the air may be a lot different than seeing for miles perched 200 feet up in an oak canopy (although in both cases, something other than you is holding you up). And the escapades of a six-year-old learning to understand and maintain her balance may not correlate to a 43-year-old intent on testing her core conditioning, tendency to act much younger than her age, or exercising her unalienable right to push the limits of someone else's liability insurance. But, does the real reason really matter? The point is that rising above one's natural height changes one's perspective. Or should.

So, tonight, I climbed a tree. Horizontally. To see what I could see in the deep well of a clear night, autumn's chill already evident. This tree has lain, since the hurricane Irene felled it, angled across my landlord's driveway, its canopy cushioned by the roof of my garage apartment. I climbed slowly, pausing in branch forks to listen to crickets, cicadas and frogs. I closed my eyes. I opened my eyes. The massive shattered trunk and exposed earth-crusted root system aft that I had found interesting and somewhat unreal in the daylight made complete primal sense to me in the darks both in and out of my mind, the awesomeness of it all finally understandable. It was a tree at least as old as I was, likely much older. A white oak that I have stared at for years. A tree that has dropped thousands of acorns in biannual autumns, falling harvests that have fattened the squirrels and dented the roof of my car. A tree whose canopy was the last thing the sun, like a sated lover, stroked at the end of the day. Whose branches, thick as trunks themselves, issued cardinals, bluejays, and goldfinches like ideas. This tree whose thundering collapse barely missed both the power lines and my head. A tree that, as I inched up its mossy northern edge, now facing south, afforded me a diorama view of my lamp-blazed bedroom, where I have had love and dreams and grieved the loss of both. Where two perplexed cats stared out, wondering why I was not the bird their eyes had tracked this morning. This tree whose fall in a hurricane named after a first love could have killed me but did not. This tree that will be memory and pieces tomorrow. I kept my balance on this tree. And no one needed to see it after all.

Paula Neves

Celerity

After a pot of smoked tea I drink trees. Green there
orange here yellow. Leaves now triangles then
grapes; round, fleshy pulses of color. Through
butternut leaves (feet playing crackles like fingers
on a flute), themselves moonlike, that bed on a
lake's rim. Lakewater a newly-minted penny.
Pumpkin-gold across everything. In a short time it's
bottom-naked in a glass. 6 PM. Thick light sucked
up quickly, as if through a straw.

up quickly, as if through a straw.
Bottom-naked in a glass. 6 PM. Thick light sucked
Pumpkin-gold across everything. In a short time it's
lake's rim. Lakewater a newly-minted penny.
on a flute), themselves moonlike, that bed on a
butternut leaves (feet playing crackles like fingers
grapes; round, fleshy pulses of color. Through
orange here yellow. Leaves now triangles then
After a pot of smoked tea I drink trees. Green there

Shira Dentz

Our Old Pond

When James Russell Lowell wrote, "And what is so rare as a day in June? / Then if ever come perfect days," it's true he was a New Englander. But he was a citified New Englander living in Cambridge, Massachusetts, in the 1840's. Did summer reach perfection there a few weeks earlier than it does in New Hampshire? I tend to gauge the season by how many times I have the courage to strip for a swim in our pond—often after a session of serious weeding in the vegetable garden that abuts it.

This pond of ours is under an acre. We had it dug in 1963 in a marshy place about 300 feet above the farmhouse, where the Soil Conservation Service had surveyed the area and laid out the perimeter. Before Ray got started with his bulldozer the soil engineers dug ten test holes to verify what they'd presumed accounted for the marsh: underground springs. In eight days the pond-to-be lay gaping open. Little by little it filled, abetted by the brook at the far end and by the rains of autumn. For what is so rare as days of fall rain, edging toward sleet, ending with snow? By the following spring our pond was full.

Ray had left a big granite rock for diving or jumping from. We decreed the surrounding area—about forty feet by sixty—the beach, which meant hauling in sand, two dump truck loads, as I recall. The impromptu rule was a dozen shovelsful before you swam. Little by little we acquired a sandy place for a few beach chairs and a barrel for cushions and goggles. True summer for me begins with those warm July days.

Last summer, you'll remember, was rainy and cold. I only got into the pond nine times before the temperature dropped in September beyond my endurance level. This year will make up for it, I hope. Fingers crossed that we won't have another algae bloom of cyanobacteria, an increasing problem in New England ponds small and large. An ingenious preventive measure to avert this problem has recently become available. It's the insertion of islands, artificial islands made of recycled water bottles and styrofoam, topped with a quantity of special soil sufficent to cover the "land mass." Since we live near a sod farm, it was easy to buy enough grass for our puny little 5 foot by 6 foot islet. Then we planted some wild water iris and black-eyed susans in the dozens of holes that dot the surface. We were advised that three islands were the correct number for our pond but since the total cost ran to just under a thousand dollars, we thought we'd try one first. We towed it out by kayak and anchored it by two concrete blocks on chains fore and aft and all last summer through the rain and mist we watched the greenery grow. The black-eyed susans bloomed merrily through October.

The vegetation of the island puts down deep roots, which tend to capture the nitrogen compounds that contribute to the formation of algae. Multiple large islands have been used successfully in the Chicago River and elsewhere to reduce pollution. So far this year, all is well. But I am writing these optimistic words in April. Three months from now, if we're lucky, we'll have an untarnished forty-odd-year-old pond awaiting us.

Maxine Kumin

"In Heaven It Is Always Autumn"
—John Donne

In heaven it is always autumn. The leaves are always near
to falling there but never fall, and pairs of souls out
　　walking
heaven's paths no longer feel the weight of years upon
　　them.
Safe in heaven's calm, they take each other's arm,
the light shining through them, all joy and terror gone.
But we are far from heaven here, in a garden ragged and
　　unkept
as Eden would be with the walls knocked down, the
　　paths littered
with the unswept leaves of many years, bright keepsakes
for children of the Fall. The light is gold, the sun pulling
the long shadow soul out of each thing, disclosing an
　　outcome.
The last roses of the year nod their frail heads,
like listeners listening to all that's said, to ask,
What brought us here? What seed? What rain? What light?
What forced us upward through dark earth? What made us
　　bloom?
What wind shall take us soon, sweeping the garden bare?
Their voiceless voices hang there, as ours might,
if we were roses, too. Their beds are blanketed with
　　leaves,
tended by an absent gardener whose life is elsewhere.
It is the last of many last days. Is it enough?
To rest in this moment? To turn our faces to the sun?
To watch the lineaments of a world passing?
To feel the metal of a black iron chair, cool and eternal,
press against our skin? To apprehend a chill as clouds
pass overhead, turning us to shivering shade and shadow?
And then to be restored, small miracle, the sun shining
　　brightly
as before? We go on, you leading the way, a figure
leaning on a cane that leaves its mark on the earth.

My friend, you have led me further than I have ever been.
To a garden in autumn. To a heaven of impermanence
where the final falling off is slow, a slow and radiant
    happening.
The light is gold. And while we're here, I think it must
    be heaven.

Elizabeth Spires

Acorn

Under its hat
many secrets
asleep
keeping time

Soon it will tell
almost everything

if you wait
long enough
in the grass in the snow

if you look if you listen

and if you do nothing
it will be what it will be
nevertheless

With a hat like that
you could walk the windiest hall
of an endless wood

as the worst and the best rain down
out of nowhere

With a hat like that
you could hide the highest hope
the biggest fear

and appear once a year to disappear

O where is the loom
on which it is woven

How can a tomb
too small for a petal
carry the body of autumn in its hull

Cradle of greenest memory

kernel dreaming
the weight of a starling

cupola cupping the fire of dawn

den of creation

shedding itself
again
for a song

O give me a room to keep a secret
until the leaf is ready
to be lit

and when it is time to go out
into the cold
give me a hat
like that

Phillis Levin

Ice Storm

Isn't it beautiful, the way the ice
holds the streets in stasis, but with glints
that flash their warnings as cautious tires roll
between the patches? You and I both wince,
consider going out, but then think twice.
Cars skid; arms break. The season takes its toll.

We're looking out from in, or there from here,
a slight or great removal from the source
of each refracted image of the chill.
I'm over here; you're over there, of course,
and if the air is frigid, it is clear
as night goes on, glittering and still.

Quincy Lehr

Bloodstone

As long as you hold me—in reverence—
whatever you want I will grant you.
Are you old? I will green you with hornblende.
If you're pink you'll be ruddled with iron.

Just put me in water and watch it
turn red like a blood revelation.
If you're frightened and faithfully drink it
you will see a dead man's resurrection.

And when you're concerned for the nation
and carve the right verses upon me
I will tear through the bindings that hurt you.
I will break down the walls that invert you.

Berlin and the wall of your wailing
were prisons that led into freedom.
I will open the door into heaven
for the body is made out of stone.

Richard Marx Weinraub

Windowless

The baby is sleeping next to the man who is no longer
    sleeping there.
All the sleeping that happens in a house, in the morning,
    when it is raining outside.
And green from all the rain outside.
The green makes the house darker than usual.
Rain makes the green light and dark, dark and light,
    luminous.
A particular light that happens in the morning when
    everyone is sleeping.
It means something to the one who sleeps.
To the one who is breathing.
But what of the one who isn't?
Some are better in the morning than others.
Some make the fact of getting up easy, others make it
    heavy.
All of these things matter.
When sleeping, when raining.
All that that dwells in the space of meaning.
Rain in the morning after a person is gone.
It seems impossible that he would not see this rain.
In July — it is dark when normally it is sunny.
It seems that the sadness of this morning is the fact that
    he is not looking out the window.
To see how the layers of green upon green make the
    whole morning dark.

Kristin Prevallet

Lightning Strike

The calm afterwards holds
a mesmerising light.
We go outside,
into the charged evening,
the palpable vibration of atoms;
down the shimmering lane,
to look for the glass dagger.

The gorse bush is charred
to its bare bones, the earth
still smouldering deep beneath
from the piercing.

Mist rises towards the moon
from the thick drenched grass
of the hayfield, where a black stag,
antlered with silver, is dreaming us.

Moyra Donaldson

First the Fan

First the fan of baseball fields, then the blotchy geometries
of farms in winter,
then the clouds, the clouds and only the clouds, this one
so thick
it's all there is to see / the clouds and the wing
with its blue triangle fin spearing out at the sky / bearing
us somehow home
to the urban mists of New York in winter.
You will go on to Maine and I will wake Christmas
morning alone / until
we meet halfway / in the in-between
where the Connecticut River splits Vermont from New
Hampshire.
I can't tell if we're still over Indiana or maybe that's
Cleveland / the captain
makes an announcement and we squint
as though we could squint the clouds clear / we pretend to
make out what's down there.

Buffalo, the captain says, Buffalo
and thirty-five to forty minutes from JFK, we found a bit
of smooth air
it may get rough later, he says, earlier he used the phrase
"bumpy air" / I like his words.
You point me to a footnote in your book; representation is
a good word
you say, we are too close to each other to write poetry and
read theory:
sprung, the footnote says, means uprising, in German,
and we are rising up / through the clouds / I point down at
Buffalo
and it looks like the snow is shimmering up through the
air with hallucinatory grace.

Snow uprising. / Snow sprung. / Sprung snow.
I'm dreaming of a White Christmas / I'm glad we're not
    going to Buffalo
a city we've been through, but it never stopped us, never
    made us shiver with awe.
I think the stewardess is too old for this job. I want to
    hold her in my arms,
make her young again. Someone's kid
screams. Someone always brings a kid that screams, to
    remind you that youth is pain.

Down there it's no longer Buffalo, now it's mountains black
    and grey,
white lines where trees were eliminated
so skiers and bears rolling down the mountains can
    make their own lines.
These landscapes are like curvy ladies
laying down beside each other, singing:
lay, lady, lay, like Bob Dylan
as they sigh and roll over and re-arrange themselves
    when no one is looking.

The wing is glinting sun like the arms of a ringmaster
    covered in rhinestones:
Behold! This land is your land / layers of imperfect rivers
    and roads and farms in fans.
When I was a child I believed these outlines were the
    outlines of states,
and all the divisions were finally revealing themselves:
there was no such thing as representation.
I can still see it now: that frozen lake is Arkansas
and there / that must be Nebraska! / I'd know that boxy
    blue wasteland anywhere.
Then America dissolves into rows of roofs and swimming
    pools
I could scrape them up with my fingernails like
    microchips.

There's the Connecticut River like a snake / so long it
    goes to the horizon rainbow
and all the way to Long Island herself, a careful fish
with the city in her eye / looking at the snake river
that wants to bite her head off
but can't seem to fit that snake-mouth around all those
    tall buildings and so many trains.
(Impossible iron spaghetti strands that can't be cut and
    too numerous to count.)
Wake up! The city is spellbound
I tell you, Look! Look at the pollution, like some sort of
    brown power
the city collects around herself. Wake up! We're here.
Circling water so low the birds
chatter at us / they watch and fly
as we swirl and we touch down.

Rena J. Mosteirin

Ways We Hold

Strange how hands can
lose their touch: unopened
jars, inexplicably split
fingernails, and casualties
from cutting bagels the wrong
way, one hand underneath
as the other slices ignobly towards it.
But I remember a better
dexterity: girls conversing
while their hands fly and fix
each other's hair; brothers playing
Heart and Soul, four hands
on a shared keyboard. All those
hands, and how they hold!
Not the nervous fellow
wringing his own, of course,
but generous hands, yours,
their round touch on each
page, and then that moment
when we rest, intertwined,
hearts pulsing even in the thumbs.

Jennifer Arin

The Scar

This is what I remember:
thirty years ago I was sitting at an oceanside café
somewhere in Spain.
The day was windy and bright. There were several of us.
An English girl was telling us about the scar
on her upper arm. Her arm was tan and brown, the scar
a shade lighter. It was a striking thing.
When she was little she had tripped
and fallen through a window.

Her name escapes me,
her face escapes me, the others at the table
are ghosts and shadows.
But the story of the scar
I remember clearly—
how for months afterwards
it spit out tiny pieces of glass,
and how it had felt, painless
but breathtaking,
like a bucket of ice water.

I think of it now, still leaping from her arm
on summer days, from t-shirts and tank-tops
after all these years, whoever she is,
wherever she is, through what life
has brought her. And I would like to believe
that if I ever saw her again
I would know her by it.

Frank Huyler

Your Kiss Is Instantaneous Dark

There is the sound of a distant engine
Breathing: A backpack leaf blower hurrying
With its bottled tones. When I open my eyes
I see the inside face of your arm, its great blue
Vein; with my ear pressed against your chest,
I hear that hum I thought was an engine.
This is what your heart sings deep inside your chest,
This song. It sounds dramatic, but I'd understand
If you traded me in for a booklet of coupons—
I'm not that good to you; I'm not very smart.
When you kiss me, it is instantaneous dark.
Even within this drought of light, there's a spot
Where a mourning dove might come to watch us steam,
Set her sight upon these confused human blocks.

Britt Melewski

Three Horses

Henceforth, three horses.
Dust- or rain-bedazzled.
Hot days or cool, days of wind
or merciful stillness, three, now, here,

three horses you must take
as long to look at as it took them
to become this triangle you could balance
a camera or lifetime or your suffering upon,

never just one horse anymore,
and never two woefully parallel horses,
but three, now, yes, three horses.
One called My Body and one called Your Body
And one called My Hooves in Your Hair.

Robin Behn

After a Fairy Tale
by Oscar Wilde

Loving the idea of love, a nightingale
pressed her breast to the thorn of a rosebush
so a rose might bloom as red as her blood.
The harder she pressed, the sweeter she sang,
until in the purest ecstasy of song,
her heart and the thorn of the rosebush met.
A man picked the rose for a woman he loved,
but the woman disdained it. The man discarded
the rose near the wheels of a cart. He went
back to his books. He forgot about love
with a valid excuse. Love, let us be neither
the man nor woman, but the nightingale:
the sharper the pain, the greater the song,
the deeper the red—the miraculous blossom.

Gardner McFall

Eclogue 2

A marriage worth of minutes we've stood
side by side, staring into the hooded depths
of your 1984 Dodge Ram pickup truck,
watching the engine chitter and die
for no apparent reason. I feel a crazy,
ignorant joy: here we go again, sweetheart,
struggling in harness over yet another
crappy mystery. Do you? I can't say I'll ever
know one way or the other what your thoughts
will do, though twenty years ago I made you cry
when I dumped you for the jerk down the hall,
and I'll never get over it, the sight of you,
cool autocrat, in tears for a dumb girl
who happened to be me.

Now I'm the one who cries all the time,
you're the one not walking away from me
down the hall. Just the same, you imagine
walking away, I'm sure of it; maybe when you're
dragging another snow-sopped log to the chainsaw
pile, or we're curled in bed waiting for a barred owl
to stammer in the pines, the barn dog shouting back
like a madwoman. It's not that being here
is misery; it's more like marriage is too much
and not enough at the same time: the trees crowd us
like children, our bodies betray a fatal longing.
What's left for us, at forty, but dismay
Till labor shakes us back into our yoke.

Work, work, that puritan duty—yet
how beautiful the set of your shoulders
when you heave a scrap of metal siding
into the trash heap. Our bodies linger
this side of lovely, like flowers under glass.
We drive ourselves to endure; on my knees

in the hay mow, stifled and panting,
I plant bale after bale in place: you toss,
you toss, I shove, I shove. We keep pace,
patient and wordless; the goats in their pen
blat irritably. In the yard our sons quarrel.
Mourning doves groan in the eaves.
Long hours ahead, till our job is done
and another begins.

Hunting scattered chickens in the bug-infested dew:
I watch you crouch along the scrubby poplar edge,
then circle back between the apple trees,
white hen skittering ahead, luminescent in the shabby
dark. Suddenly she drops her head and sits,
submissive as a girl. You've got her now; tuck up her feet
and carry her back home, then squat to mend the ragged fence.
A breath of sweat rises from your sunburnt neck,
salt and sweet. My love. Marry me, I say. You cast
an eye askance and shrug, I did. How odd it seems
that this is where we've landed: chasing chickens
through the woods at twilight, humid thunder rumpling
the summer sky, dishes washed, a slice of berry pie left
cooling on the counter. I've been saving it for you.

Dawn Potter

The Art of Giving

You were my favorite—
Aran Irish wool
eight buttons—
lent to a friend
who was boarding a chilly plane
after a weekend visit.
She promised to ship you back.
That was two years ago.
I never ask for you
but I know exactly where you are.

Kathleen Gerard

I Have Eagerly Desired to Eat
This Passover with You

A table I prepare for you
Once and for all
The nights I cannot remain

For the meals you eat alone
For the cups run dry
For all the lack

Come drink, come feast
Come
You will always have enough

Elizabeth Kim

Southern Comfort

Whiskey on the rocks. That was my dad's evening drink. As a girl, I liked to hold my father's glass, feel the cold against my face, then lift it up so I could see the light coming through the liquid, golden like the hairs on my father's arms, like Triscuits and the meadow that stretched out behind the barn. Sometimes I'd sip it, and if Mom was out of town, Dad would serve me my own drink, mixing lemon, sugar, whiskey and water, letting me taste the fire on my tongue, throat, and deep inside. *Does it burn you, Daddy?* No, he'd say. Not with just one drink. Then he'd pour himself another one to *take the edge off the day*. And I'd watch it happen, the edges of the day dissolving, everything that had been the day moving away from us, no longer true or obvious like the black and white of the clock hands moving toward bedtime. When at last it was dark and late, and all that was left were two pools of lamplight, tiny 40-watt islands, just for us, my father reading on the couch, me on my belly, head cocked sideways, staring at picture books I'd read a thousand times, I'd play a game in my mind, trying to hold on to that moment, make it last, just a little longer, and pretend, this is all there is. Just this, this whiskey light, the two of us alone, together, on a summer night.

Nin Andrews

First Flight

Champagne. Always champagne. Even David
who does not drink will toast the flight's success.
The new initiate doused with it will
know its flowing tingle over the skin
not unlike the wind that so recently
moved the balloon, all its eight hundred pounds
(exclusive of human freight), so lightly
up and through the sky, less miraculous
than the bumblebee, but no less fragile,
its one wing of nylon and Hyperlife,
that must not burn or tear or twist too much,
but bounce like a bubble on the currents
of air until it can be set down square
and safe as the champagne waits to pop.

Marta Ferguson

Bliss

I will arise and go now, and go to Innisfree,
And a small cabin build there, of clay and wattles made;
Nine bean rows will I have there, a hive for the honey bee,
And live alone in the bee-loud glade.

—William Butler Yeats

My great grandfather, Fleming Jefferson Davis, grew fruit trees in central Kentucky, on the road halfway between Grab and Donansburg, two orchards to be exact, with Lincoln pears, Elberta peaches, and all manner of apples, including Red Junes, Maiden Blush, Sapsucker, and Northern Spy. With so many blossoms to tend, none of which could bear fruit unless pollinated, he also kept bees.

Passion ought to be fragrant, don't you think, trussed up like a young girl trying to catch her date's attention at the first high school dance? But in this section of Kentucky virtually every Davis was born, raised, and died a Separate Baptist, which meant that passion and pleasure and dancing were suspect.

Can you imagine spring in those orchards: white and pink blossoms thrown to the ends of branches like confetti, the faint syrupy smell of possibility, and the sound of bees everywhere? I've often wondered if this was the way my Puritan ancestors winked at God, immersing themselves in the radical abundance of nature, cultivating it under the auspices of agriculture so no one would dare damn this profusion of sensual delights.

If you've never been stung, or if you've been stung but got over the fear of the swelling pinprick to recognize its necessity in keeping the world spinning, then you know the movement of bees should hold no dread, that their dance may be the most beautiful to witness, if you're willing to take the time to lie under the trees, head turned to the sky and to the profusion of blossoms that appear to hold the heavens in their rightful place.

There's a fluidity to bee flight, a languid rhythm to their comings and goings. Nothing overly choreographed: part ballet, part waltz. No tango or salsa here, despite their costuming and their tiny bee hips swaying back and forth in provocation.

Yet there's no denying that this dance—despite its loveliness, its bodily gratification—bears a purpose. A certain kind of love drives these creatures in their persistence, enabling their single-minded vision. Who can glimpse the pollen these bees store on their legs—so sticky and heavy at times that flight becomes difficult—without confessing an odd passion stirring the blood? Who can hear the hum of what Yeats called a bee-loud glade and not remember the thirst of one's yearning for this solace, a constant craving to taste the sugar of this world's offering, to drink until full, then to move on to another flower, only to thirst again?

I wonder if my great grandfather considered such matters. I know my grandfather and father did on their walks at the Pierce farm, listened to them philosophizing about the woods, about the absurdity of plentitude and lack, and so it's my birthright to ask, Where did this dancing lead? What was the conclusion of this bee-laden love-making, this world-making, which took place in a remote orchard nearly a century ago?

Some of those rhythms culminated in the waxen comb which Fleming would slice with a butcher knife: whetted edge dripping with honey the color of a wheat field, the bees having fled from the clouds he poured out of his kettle-shaped smoker. Yes, bee-dancing brought the hive's harvest, but it also went into the making of a white peach my father now can't remember the name for, a fruited ecstasy he's scoured farm stands, garden catalogs, and produce aisles in search of for the past 60 years with no luck.

He says that particular kind of peach was large and came on in July when the heat was beginning to weigh on everyone. He's told me that slicing into one of those midsummer globes, watching the paring knife undo the velvet of its skin and the first drop of juice sliding down onto the thumb's tip was pure pleasure, a sanctioned hedonism that could not be overturned despite the church's best efforts. It was summer's hellish heat undone by a bliss that tasted like honey tinged with apples and pears, a sweetness that was like staring at the sun through the leaves while kissing a girl from the next farm over who kissed you back even harder.

Todd Davis

Beets

I think they must be very old,
holding fast for years in a tight cold place,
escaping the scythe through sheer
homeliness.

They wobble on my cutting board,
big awkward knobs smelling
of rain-soaked soil, sparse hairs
trailing from greyed, misshapen domes.
Just to see them makes me feel younger today.

When I boil and slice them open
I find a tree's concentric rings
closing into one tiny secret core.
Peeled, their skin is smooth as a youth's
and radiant.

I love the way they yield their essence
with such ease,
surprising me the way my gashed knee
surprised me as a child.

We are lively, they say, vibrant,
not at all what you thought.
Let us mark you with our brilliance,
spiral scarlet over your fingers,
stain your hands with our sweet ageless blood.

I want to carry their stain for days.

Maria Terrone

Ode to Chocolate

I hate milk chocolate, don't want clouds
of cream diluting the dark night sky,
don't want pralines or raisins, rubble
in this smooth plateau. I like my coffee
black, my beer from Germany, wine
from Burgundy, the darker, the better.
I like my heroes complicated and brooding,
James Dean in oiled leather, leaning
on a motorcycle. You know the color.

Oh, chocolate! From the spice bazaars
of Africa, hulled in mills, beaten,
pressed in bars. The cold slab of a cave's
interior, when all the stars
have gone to sleep.

Chocolate strolls up to the microphone
and plays jazz at midnight, the low slow
notes of a bass clarinet. Chocolate saunters
down the runway, slouches in quaint
boutiques; its style is *je ne sais quoi*.
Chocolate stays up late and gambles,
likes roulette. Always bets
on the *noir*.

Barbara Crooker

The Little Red Hen and Abuelita

The Little Red Hen was hungry. There was nothing in the pantry but refried beans and cheese. She called her husband, Rocky, at his office.

"Rocky Roofing," he said. "Something to crow about!"

"Crowing, shmowing," she said. "There's nothing to eat!"

"Call my grandmother," Rocky said. "My abuelita knows everything."

So she did.

"Make pupusas!" Abuelita said. "Here's the recipe."

The Little Red Hen frowned, looking at her watch. "Who will buy the masa harina? I'm too busy for that."

"I will!" said Abuelita. She ran to the market. When she got to the house, the Little Red Hen was working at the computer. So Abuelita unpacked the bags and tiptoed out.

Soon the Little Red Hen called again. "About the pupusas," she said, tapping her foot. "Who'll make the dough? I'm too busy for that."

"I will!" said Abuelita. She grabbed her mixing bowl. When she got to the house, the Little Red Hen was fixing the bathroom sink. So Abuelita mixed and kneaded until she had a pile of dough and tiptoed out.

The Little Red Hen called again. "About the pupusas," she said, pacing back and forth. "Who'll add the fillings? I'm too busy for that."

"I will!" said Abuelita. She packed her rolling pin. When she got to the house, the Little Red Hen was upstairs helping the children with their homework. So Abuelita spooned in cheese and refried beans, folded up the sides, flattened them and tiptoed out.

The Little Red Hen called again. "About the pupusas," she said, clucking her tongue. "Who'll cook them? I'm too busy for that."

"I will!" Abuelita said. She found her frying pan. When she got to the house, the Little Red Hen was napping with the baby—and a pile of laundry—on the couch.

"Puuu-puu-sasss," she said, talking in her sleep.

So Abuelita fried and flipped the dough. Then she tiptoed out—and hid beneath and open window.

After the Little Red Hen woke up, she watered the lawn, vacuumed the house and drove the children to soccer practice.

When Rocky came home from work, the Little Red Hen danced the salsa as she carried a tray of pupusas. She fluffed her feathers and cooed. "I shopped and mixed and kneaded and filled and cooked and flattened and fried and flipped. I did it all myself!"

Rocky rubbed his stomach. "Sweet," he said. "Let's eat!"

So they did.

Suddenly, there was a knock at the door.

"Abuelita!" Rocky said. "What a surprise! Join us for dinner."

But there were no pupusas left.

"Don't worry about me," Abuelita said. "I'll just sit and rest awhile."

With that, the Little Red Hen grabbed her dancing shoes with one hand and Rocky's collar with the other.

"Mi casa es tu casa. Make yourself comfortable," Rocky said, on his way out.

"Not *too* comfortable," the Little Red Hen muttered under her breath.

And, at that moment, Abuelita almost told the truth about that Little Red Hen.

But when she looked out the window, she saw the Little Red Hen and her grandson dancing cheek to cheek and very much in love.

So who do you think washed the dishes, wiped the table, swept the floor and took out the garbage so they would come home to a nice, clean house?

Don't ask.

Which is just what Abuelita told the Little Red Hen the next time she called.

Because a grandmother can be very busy herself.

Abuelita's Recipe for Pupusas
(pronounced *poo-POO-sahs*)

2 cups masa harina
1 cup water
1 cup filling (for example, cheese, pork rinds, or refried beans)

1. Mix together the masa harina and water. Knead to make a dough.
2. Roll the dough into 8 small balls.
3. Press a hole in each ball with your thumb. Put one tablespoon of filling into each ball.
4. Fold the dough over so the filling doesn't fall out.
5. Flatten the balls with your hands or with a rolling pin.
6. Cook each pupusa on a preheated ungreased skillet for for a minute or two until lightly browned. (Ask an adult for help—the skillet is hot!)

Pupusas taste good with coleslaw and tomato sauce.

Janice Levy

Collecting Spanishes

Abuelita's English was just like her
bread pudding punctuated with raisins
nobody ever asked for. Condensed milk
contradictions, fattening tenses,
cinnamon questions and eggshell promises.

Papi's Spanish was a group of poets
workshopping. Not overly concerned
with agreement and never without purpose.
I don't ever remember him
speaking in Ñ's to me but I loved him most
when he spent all his accents on Momma.

Momma's Spanish was slow-moving
silkworms which sometimes threaded
stars into Greek myth and lullaby.
Other times they tangled words
into ivy wrapping up a building brick by brick.

Abuelo's Spanish folded itself into English
tea sandwiches. Cucumber and watercress
covered in adobo y habichuela negra.
I never tasted the recipe. He wasn't around often
enough for them to be prepared
and something like that doesn't keep well.

Roberto F. Santiago

Yollie's Rice

No amount of salt can save the bowl of rice in front of me.
This meal would have once been adequate, even tasty.

That was before eating my mother-in-law's moro,
A flawless Chiaroscuro of frijoles negro y arroz blanco

So perfectly sweet there is nearly no need for dessert.
Now no one else's rice can possibly be taken seriously.

When I praise her gastronomical Matisse,
She shyly smiles and the eight-year-old Yolanda

Peaks out from underneath her seventy-year-old face.
I recognize this same smile hanging

From my wife's visage whenever Chicago
House music pulses from a stereo.

"The rice is too dry," she dissents,
Always quick to deflate a compliment,

Another trait inherited by her daughter.
In her immense modesty she is monumentally wrong;

Somewhere in the world there are rice grains growing in
    a field
And they are all praying to end up in the grace of Yollie's
    cupboard.

As her daughter has ruined me for all other women,
Yolanda has ruined me for all other rice.

Vincent Toro

The Inheritance

Just a grapefruit
but it never fails
to make the word *Mama*
when I cut it,
store the half uneaten
flat against a plate,
pink meat down
so that tomorrow
when I eat it it's as juicy
as today. Washing fruit
she taught us but never this.
She just did it. Saved
the fruit against the plate.
As I do. As I saw it done
in my daughter's house this morning.

Myra Shapiro

Seeing in the Dark

"Would you like to go outside and see the darkness?" I ask her.

She is intrigued but on guard. It is already late. "But how will we see?" she asks.

"Lots of ways," I tell her. "We'll take a flashlight for sure. Maybe we'll see lightning bugs."

"Lightning bugs?" she says quickly, with a deep breath. She's curious. She's hooked.

Then she remembers. "But, Nana, I don't like the darkness. I can't see in the dark."

"Come on," I say, taking her hand. "I'll show you how to see in the dark."

We cross the threshold. She's only three and usually long asleep in bed by this time. We stand on the doorstep and I tell her to watch the air with her eyes wide open. We'll accustom our eyes till we begin to see things we didn't think we could see. Her hand tightens its hold on mine, her eyes widen.

The air is silky and warm. We are surrounded by the sound of tree frogs chirping in the darkness. My eyes adjust to the half light and I tell her, almost whispering, how I can already see the little pebbles on the driveway that looks like a wide white path . . . and the trunks of trees growing up, the white birch. . . .

"Yes," she begins, "I see the branches. I can see the grass!"

"Shall we walk down the driveway?" I ask her, even as we move out away from the house with its windows glowing behind us. It feels as if we are entering some special place. The front yard has been transformed. The starry sky a canopy over our heads, over the tree tops out farther than we can see. She thinks there could be foxes and bears in the woods beyond us.

I look down at this little daughter of my daughter standing next to me in the dark. The moment is suddenly, unexpectedly weighted. It's as if I can see the air and see through the air, hear the whisperings of generations before us and all those to come after.

Stones crunch under our feet. She spots the moon, the milky, luminous moon so big and so round right there on the top of the tallest tree branch. She wants to shine the flashlight so we make little moons, little circles of light on the ground, against the trees, in the air. We watch what was invisible become visible—a patch of grass, the bit of wind catching leaves—that's where the rustling sound is coming from. There's the wind chime. . . .

Just as our eyes become accustomed to the shadows, our ears begin to listen for the different night noises: grasshoppers, katydids, tree frogs, the single notes of the wind chime rise and disappear.

We see few lightning bugs, but enough. She gets to see the twinkling lights blink their message of light in a kind of insect version of the "Here Where" game. Summer evenings when I was a kid we played it in the half dark after dinner. The one who was "It" closed her eyes or was blindfolded. The others spread themselves around the yard calling, "Here," "Here." The finder listened to locate the voices, then called back, "Where?" and waited for an answering "Here" before running after the sound. When you were caught you became the next seeker in this version of "Hide and Seek." The sense of what we couldn't see, sounds bobbling, nested, rustling, that excitement and anticipation, running, sticks crackling underfoot, almost out of breath, "Where?" "Here," "Where?"

Having a grandchild is like being found. It's as if, totally unbeknownst to me, I'd been calling, "Here, here," and all the while the unseen was answering, "Where, where?" There's a physicality not unlike someone touching you in the darkness, like being tagged, found, that weight of this newborn in your arms.

"Nana, tell me about the jars," she says.

She remembers the story of how my sister and I ran barefoot after dinner catching lightning bugs in our bare hands. We put them in jelly jars. We pierced small round holes in the tops so the bugs could breathe. We carried the jars around the yard like small lanterns, the little triangles of neon blinking on off on off. Bug feet and bug wings tickled my palms as I held them waiting for my sister to open the jar. It had to be quick. I had to cup my hands together tight enough to keep the lighting bug from getting away but not so tight it got squashed. She opened the lid just enough to put the new one in. Quick, close it. We filled the jars with light then opened them again and let them go.

Like tonight, grass already gathering dew, I'm full to overflowing, full of the completeness of being here, night time with its dazzle of sights and sounds, with my granddaughter discovering such ordinary magic. We breathe it in. Her face radiant as a small moon. She wants to sing and we turn toward the house singing her song into the night.

Susan Jackson

My Brother Stands in the Snow, 1947, Paterson, NJ

Fifty years later, my brother is still my baby brother.
I imagine him in his woolen winter coat, tan-colored,
that with his sallow face made him look dead,
and his woolen hat that matched the coat. It had ear
flaps that snapped under his chin. He is about four
and looks wide-eyed and sweet and even then,
self-contained. I can see him standing in the snow.

It is 1947, that huge snowstorm where the snow is piled
almost to my chest. Even fifty years later, my brother
who has now been a doctor for more than thirty years,
is still my baby brother. Though he is my doctor, though I
admire and love him, though his hair has turned gray,
I can hear my mother's voice telling me to watch out
for him, as my sister watched out for me,
so that even today, I can't help worrying about him,

can't help reaching up to smooth down his thinning gray
hair when it is rumpled and fly-away, as though he were still
that little boy whose hair I combed so carefully, wetting
the comb first and parting the hair as my mother taught me
so he'd look good when people saw him on the street
where I dragged him behind me, held his hand
and scolded him as we walked.

Maria Mazziotti Gillan

My Mother Had Red Hair

My mother had red hair. My mother said put yourself in the other person's place. My mother took me to the bakery and let me pick out cookies. My mother tucked me in. My mother said it would be okay. My mother had a father who painted houses. My mother felt better with her lipstick on my mother died. My mother held my hand. My mother liked to sit in the garden my father planted. My mother painted gardens. My mother knew what I was thinking before I said it my mother gave me sisters. My mother asked the piano teacher for the Beatles instead of Mozart. My mother told me I was not allowed to hate. My mother read me Peter Pan. My mother didn't know that she was beautiful. My mother said to me "Do what you have to do." My mother never raised her voice. My mother liked boys with long hair my mother had red hair that everyone thought was dyed. My mother kept all her friends from childhood my mother loved her students. My mother said get rid of the guilt. My mother never told me to turn down the music my mother packed my lunch. My mother told me I would know it when I fell in love. My mother said "How can I let you go home?!" My mother helped me tie-dye a shirt. My mother said "Sal!!" when I called on the phone. My mother wanted to be a ballet dancer. My mother felt better with her lipstick on. My mother asked what makes this a poem. My mother didn't know that she was beautiful. My mother told me it would be okay. My mother had red hair my mother held my hand my mother died my mother tucked me in. I put my mother's lipstick on My mother my mother my mother my mother my mother.

Sally Lipton Derringer

Living with the Dead

My mother speaks of a mother,
She cannot remember,
Who died before her infant
Memory took shape,
The only relics left:
An unstrung wooden rosary, and
A patched *mantilla* of black lace.

Her mother's legacy of
Jewel-encrusted rings and brooches,
Taffeta dresses of the finest silks,
Along with the contents of her hope chest,
Might as well have been scattered to the winds.

Divided among four wailing sisters
Who would not relinquish
Their loving memory,
So greedy in their grief,
They did not stop to think
To console her stricken widower
Left alone to mind their infant niece.

My father spoke of a father,
All he could do
Was to remember,
Surrounded by mementos,
Photos, books and art.

Seeing his father's face
In his own reflection
When he shaved
Must have daily ripped his heart.

It is this same face that I carry
That stirred my mother's
Rage and sorrow
Too soon after my father's heart
Finally gave way.
This man I once cherished
Whose apparition I now strive to stave away.

It wakes me from my dreams,
Each fitful night,
To remind me of another—
One who has forgotten
The future and her presence
Buried under memories
Of past delight.

You see, to my mother
I have become
Her daughter's daughter.
She asked me why her daughter
Never comes to see her,
Why her own husband doesn't care,
Forgetting that I never had a daughter,
That my father's long departed,
Never knowing
It is I who strokes her hair.

Roxanne Hoffman

I Imagine My Father's Dying Request

Please, keep these letters safe.
They are written by my three lovers
(none your mother or my dear wife).
I know all of them by heart,
the last letter from each so sad
I like to believe I received these first,
not as prologue but as pardon,
our endings forgiven
before we began.
Now here I am in a hospital bed
in the middle of my living room,
unable to move and forgetting everything;
yes, so close to the end you'd be safe to write it.
Go ahead—write it. Then tell my story backwards.
Write about the day I learned I had cancer.
Write about the day before.

Mark Brazaitis

Throwing Chalk

I can see him well from where I am sitting. He stands by the modest classroom doorway. Of course. He had picked that exact spot in this tiny classroom in which his students sit watching him. He had picked that exact spot, picking up a yellow chalk at the blackboard he now holds in his right hand. The chalk lies softly on his palm now, and before he gazes momentarily at it, he is already aware of its presence. How it felt, I don't suppose I know, but chalk is chalky, and everything begins with that in this class. He has a chalk in his right hand, and he is going to throw that chalk up, and he is going to catch it. He seems so relaxed. I cannot see a smile, and his eyes drift farther away. He focuses on the chalk. There is a pause in his movements. He prepares himself to begin. He prepares himself to move. He lowers his right hand and lifts it up again, imparting measured movement into the chalk. The chalk disengages, slowly losing contact with his hand. I can see the chalk lifting into the air. I can see him gaze at the chalk as it departs from his hand. I can see him move towards the chalk. I can count his movements. I can feel the measured pace. He takes one step forward. The chalk is still being propelled upwards, but its pace is slower now, and it will reach a peak height in which all its momentum will be spent, and then gravity will pull it down again. He knows the distance between the chalk and his hand. He keeps his right palm open, to blanket the chalk's fall when it does fall again. He takes another step, a small one, almost like the step he had taken before. His footsteps fall softly on the ground. The chalk makes no noise. He keeps sight of the chalk before him. He lifts his head up slightly, but his eyes are drawn higher as the chalk makes a loop in the air and turns to fall back down. He takes just one more small step. He stops. The chalk is falling. He raises his palm and brings it slightly forward, and he waits for contact. The chalk falls. His palm is just slightly lowered as the chalk is brought back to his palm again, so it makes a soft, quiet landing. He breathes.

Joanne Chin

I'm True

my six year old says,
meaning I'm telling the truth.

I correct him in the way fathers
are supposed to: *you should
really say I'm telling the truth.*

But he shakes his head, folds
arms tight across his chest and says,
no Dad, I'm true, really, I'm true.

I start to correct him again, then
catch myself, say, *yes, I know
Trevor, you are true.*

Steve Cushman

The Truth Fairy

Having the most liberal parents in my neighborhood, by six I had already debunked God, the stork, and Santa Claus. To strident cries of "Nut-u-u-uh," I announced the mashing together of the "downthere's" of all kids' parents. "That's how they planted the seed of you that grew inside your mother," I told them, "And if you don't believe me just sneak into your parents' bedroom the next time you hear animal sounds coming from there." I may have been an atheist, but I was on a mission. Next on my list to unmask was the Tooth Fairy.

She was the only modern mythological figure in whom it would have behooved me to believe. I'm not sure why, but my parents had been mum on the subject, dutifully exchanging quarters and dollars in the night for my older brother's cast-off teeth. Although I myself was eager to amass piggy bank wealth, the hypocrisy of my family's capitulation to the Tooth Fairy myth irked me. For the sake of truth and for that of the kids in my neighborhood, I longed to disabuse the world of the lie of the Tooth Fairy. This crusade could, however, prove difficult as, at six, I hadn't yet lost a tooth nor was there the slightest wiggle in my jaw.

A first-grade classroom is a virtual carnival of loose teeth. Knowing this, I marched myself to school, my twenty-four little pearly whites firmly in my head. I'd need a plan. All I had to do was secure myself a tooth. Then, unbeknownst to my parents, I'd stash the contraband beneath my pillow only to wake up the next day to . . . the tooth—no money, no pixie dust or whatever other remnants the Tooth Fairy was supposed to leave. I'd bring the tooth to school the following day and show it as evidence of the Tooth Fairy defrocked.

Unfortunately, nobody was losing a tooth in my class on the day of my planned crusade—the teacher was in the habit of announcing that sort of thing. So my only option was the automatic refuge of all children: wishing. As hard as I could, I wished. During independent reading period, I beamed silently into the air to no one in particular: "Please, please, please, I nee-ee—ed a tooth for my project." I squeezed my eyes shut for the longest moment I could, and when I opened them, to my absolute astonishment, there on the orange carpeting, before my Mary Jane encased toe, sat a little chip of bone. Oh, but it couldn't be a tooth. That would be too rich. I'd never had a wish come true before. I squatted and scooped it up. Lo and behold—it was a perfect little bicuspid. My hand snapped shut around the treasure. My blood surged like a roller coaster inside me, and I felt it plunging me down the most thrilling slope. I stifled my shriek.

As casually as possible, I made my way to my little desk. I pretended to search for an eraser in my arts and crafts box, depositing the tooth beneath a pile of pilfered felt ducks and apples. By recess the tooth was safely stowed in the arts and crafts box, shoved deep inside my desk.

The recess yard was huge, rife with opportunities to spill my guts. There were the hopscotch courts—where my friends invited me to play, a rowdy jump rope game where I could have both determined my future husband (doctor, lawyer, beggar man, thief) and regaled the girls with the tale of my petite miracle, the honeysuckle fence—where I usually met my old kindergarten pals. Nevertheless, I chose to orbit the outer edge of the playground, not speaking to a soul. My debunking crusade could be ruined by one false slip of the tongue.

Back in the classroom, I worked hard at forgetting the exciting manifestation of the tooth and the prospect of defrocking the Tooth Fairy. I didn't check that the tooth was still in my arts and crafts box. I didn't talk to anyone till the bell rang at three o'clock, at which point, I dove into my desk to withdraw the precious bone. I stacked my workbooks on top of my desk, dug out the arts and crafts box, and ceremoniously opened it. I lifted the felt ducks, the apples to find . . . nothing. The tooth had vanished.

It took me years to realize that my mission had not

been simply botched by bad luck. For it dawned on me that the most logical and interested party to perform such a miracle as the revelation and subsequent disappearance of a tooth wished for to disprove her existence would be none other than the Tooth Fairy.

Tamra Plotnick

Around, In, and Under Her Bed

Hand blown blue-gray glass beads escape,
roll off a braid, lavender twine
I knotted for a little wrist.
Calico sticks to a block of pine,

six china kittens curl below
one of her boyfriend's white crew socks,
lipsticks, a black suede driving glove,
yellow silk scarf still in the box.

We form a family of keepers—
way at the back, under her bed
two sleeping streets of trees and houses
lie, replete with stories. Red

gambrels, scuffed trucks layer a midden
so many childhood years in the making.
This week she wears a plastic nametag,
checks off the courses she is taking.

As the class of 2010 lies down
in long-twin beds, I sift, excise,
I dig to rediscover two
blue beads the color of her eyes.

Dolores Hayden

Mommy, What Is the Train Asking About?

Somewhere on the other side
of this long sunlight
and the match-flare leaves
the train thinks it's alive,
shapes the sound
fading away from it
into the same question
over and over.
And because the stones are warm
in fields golden-poured
around purple vetch,
and streams are quivering
around the elegance of frogs,
I believe that this sound
is a lingering—
not a hope for pity
nor a naming of loss.

Melissa Carl

Trout Quintet

Parked in the driveway, we sit in the car,
the archaeologist, who was my father,
and I, listening
to *The Trout Quintet* on the radio.
We will hear it out
on this January afternoon
as the heat flows up
through the car's roof—
in piano bubbles
of fish.

All day he tells his stories
even when he can't remember
our names. He gazes inward
at the tessarae
of his life. I listen
as I think a fish might.
We are of the same school—
my father and I—
but have no memories
of each other's life.

Today I hear again
of when, as a small boy,
he saw a drowned man
pulled from a lake,
the body's marbled limbs
streaming, the head flung back.

Today I hear again
of the mosaic below
the dusty surface of a Roman field:
Hylas, Herakles' darling boy,
and two nymphs pulling him down
for his beauty into cool waters where
he knelt to drink.

In the car my father weeps.
The cello plumbs the bottom
of a pool. Trout flicker
like shards of glass and disappear.
We grope our way to the surface,
arriving breathless on the final notes.

Martha Oliver-Smith

For a Taxi Driver Named Comfort, Las Vegas

Is she still there, her taxi reeking
of pine-scented air freshener, trawling
the Strip for fares as the sun retires
to let the neon glow take over its shift?

Is she still there, who ferried me through
that strange prosthetic town, and why is it
after all these years I should remember
so well her broad shoulders hunched

in her tense gripping of the steering wheel,
her deep voice burdened with knowledge?
Despite dozens of cities, countless drivers
since, despite the roads I've propelled myself

along, why is it her to whom I offer this
simple gesture of remembrance, and why
do I pray for her who simply carried me
when my blistered, unsteady feet could not?

Bernadette Geyer

John Lennon Glasses

don't imagine the chalk
outline of his body but saffron
handprints my nephews
etch on driveways, bright
beaks of ducklings, the delicate
daffodil & peace we squander
because it feels somehow
false & simple like a coupon
& there's no crimson thumbprint
swirled against the lens only
the Yes of a world
unfuzzed, having seen so much
poetry & terror which is
an accurate summary of our lives
on jackhammer migraine days
gusting hail when dynamite
roars through the sacred
guts of churches or just
poetry & terror in the cubicle
on days we crave sky after the subway's
long claustrophobia beneath
gravestones & angled pipes & perhaps
you pass me in the crosswalk
as its timer blinks from green
to orange, only seconds left
before the red palm strands
all the leather briefcases
& you fumble yours, papers splattering
so together we gather what we can
while taxis shriek their horns
at two strangers on their knees

Adam Tavel

The Ardabil Carpet

I saw effulgence:
a spoked comet,
its subject stars
prostrated.
The world made
anew, its yellow
monarch spinning
in viridian stillness.

"Unknown" whether
this lustre lay on
mosque or palace
floor. From
the glass case, all
are beckoned.

Natania Rosenfeld

The Flaw

The best thing about a hand-made pattern
is the flaw.
Sooner or later in a hand-loomed rug,
among the squares and flattened triangles,
a little red nub might soar above a blue field,
or a purple cross might sneak in between
the neat ochre teeth of the border.
The flaw we live by, the wrong color floss,
now wreathes among the uniform strands
and, because it does not match,
makes a red bird fly,
turning blue field into sky.
It is almost, after long silence, a word
spoken aloud, a hand saying through the flaw,
I'm alive, discovered by your eye.

Molly Peacock

A Poem for the Reader to Finish

for Jason

When it is getting dark, these deep-blue summer evenings,
it seems it never will be dark,
that the silver river must hold its shine
and the man fishing in the middle
with waters tumbling around him
will never have to stand where there is no light.
That the green hills will stand gray-green forever
and the deer won't draw a blanket of darkness over them.

I believe I could drive on till morning,
holding the darkness all the way back—
but the gray is falling heavily,
like rain, and soon it is too late.
If I am lucky, tomorrow will bring new light.
If I am lucky, tonight will be a peaceful night.
And if we are very lucky. . . .

Liz Rosenberg

Aftermath

Dawn. The moment it was
it was over.
—Deborah Tall

It was that last, euphoric summer, between
one chemo and another, when you looked out
your kitchen window and saw the doe standing
at the edge of your lawn where the thicket gathers—
autumn olive, buckthorn, forsythia, dogwood.
And when you stepped outside, the doe stayed still
and looked in your eyes, you thought, with a companionable
complicit question, and didn't run. You were
light-headed. The doe lowered her nose
to shove at the small bundle at her feet
folded up like an awkward deck chair
till then invisible in its hollow of grass.
She had just given birth. The fawn couldn't stand
but raised its too-large head to gaze at you.
You were, as you said, already more or less
posthumous. You took each other in.
One of you before, the other beyond fear.
Two creatures, side effects on one another,
headed in opposite directions.

Rosanna Warren

standing at the shore

afterwards we will
look at it and say
this was when we still or
this was before
but then we will not be
at that same soft moment
grouped in pastel shirts
the children giddy with being
on the beach at nearly bedtime
digging their toes into the sand
wild to escape to the waves
get their clothes wet
looking back we may see
the messy instant of everyone
trying to be perfect or
we may see it
framed by then
glowing
that minute
when we did not know where
we would be looking back from

Ellen Steinbaum

Breaktide

Buoyancy

was
lungs.

Lungs

were
nuisance.

Nuisance
bloomed

a
wave which

bloomed

a
lake.

The
lake

receded.

Silvering
out to shore

a
single shiver.

I scavenged

breaktide
silver,

braced

for thermocline.

Scavenger's
daughter

washed
up

like
a safe thing.

Washed
of scathe, forgetful

of
balance.

Treading

where
waves were striking.

Angel

of
incidence,

angel
of scant reflection:

This

which
was my home

is
not my home.

Krenhook,
in hand,

I drifted,

silvering
scavenge

of
breaktide

harrow.

Michael Snediker

Throwing It

Throwing the glitter for the dog
in the dark, on the overgrown lot,
smell of pittosporum—sweet, unbeautiful,
rolling over me like a cloud

and the ball vanishes into
the trees, the dog after it,
it emerges, seeming to bounce
on its own, coming toward you

glittering, the black dog only
a darker shadow. Is this not
contentment, the dog, the night,
the ball, the sense of motion

in stillness, your arm drawn back
once more, the bright globe in your hand,
a panting in the darkness at your feet
and in the sky Orion, Cassiopeia?

Janet McCann

Walking Holly down a Wooded Lane

I've tried sneaking by the house
next door, not to wake
Holly from her sphinx-pawed sleep.

I don't know how to be
with the joy in her clinking tags
soon after I round

the corner of her drive—
the tongue-lolling beast
galloping behind me,

ears back, tail whipping.
Decades, now, since I rescued
a retriever, like her, beaten

in the street. I lived
in an apartment, so I placed her
on a farm. I still think of her,

and all the lovers, family, friends
who were not to be, for lack of
time, or courage, or means.

What have I abandoned
that Holly should so surprise me?
I turn and call to this golden creature.

I won't walk as many hills:
she might bolt into the road
when we've passed these woods,

or her people might come home
and catch us in this mutual
kidnapping. Yesterday, I

stole past.
Halfway down the lane
I hear her *clink-clink*ing:

Love knows when we're
trying to slip away, and follows—
regardless—then takes the lead.

Susanna Rich

My Dog Grandma

My grandmother loved dogs
She had five
She said when she died she would come back as a dog

When grandma was very ill
Each member of the family took one dog
My mother had enough of grandma's nonsense

Grandma died
On the day she was buried
A dog scratched and howled at our door
My mother said,
"Shoo, shoo, shoo"

I was nine years old
Grandma always said she was coming back as a dog
Mama stopped in her tracks

Grandma
Grandma
I called the dog

We kept Grandma for nine wonderful years. . . .

Vincent J. Tomeo

The Gallaghers' Goat

Our country neighbor Rich Gallagher was an artist, a serious oil painter who was always winning awards. He taught art at an area high school.

"All I want to do is paint," he once told me. His wife Anne believed in his considerable talent, which she seemed to encourage by refusing to get pregnant. She was an affable blonde, nearly as tall as Rich.

Given his teaching schedule, Rich, like me, had the summers off. Not so Anne, who worked somewhere in town. And yet we rarely saw Rich out in the yard. He was always in his studio, one of the back bedrooms that caught the best light. Rich was so obsessed with painting that he wasn't much of a man-around-the-house, leaving the indoor tasks to Anne and the outdoor tasks—such as cutting their acre of grass—to themselves.

Which is why he bought a goat, a frisky goat with two horns that swept back from the top of its head like small bananas. It was the kind of goat you see in children's books, right down to the hair on its chinny-chin-chin.

"How d' ya like my new lawn mower?" Rich said was we met at the mailbox one morning. He had tethered his goat with a length of clothesline to the kind of stake used for playing horseshoes, giving it the freedom to graze across the entire front yard. He figured he'd change the location of that stake every few days, keeping the grass trim all around the property. Which would leave him ample time for his painting.

The goat, at first, didn't cooperate. Being a rather young goat, it jumped around a lot, kicking its heels. But eventually it got the message and got down to work. It wasn't long, however, before the kids on the ridge—a ragamuffin bunch of rascals and munchkins—discovered the goat and flocked to the Gallaghers' yard to taunt it. But that didn't last long. Because when Michael Moran, the oldest and toughest of the kids, dared to come close, the Gallaghers' goat lowered its head as if to butt him, and all the kids fled, with Michael leading the way.

That's what we called it—the Gallaghers' goat—because Rich and Anne never gave it a name. They never got a chance to because they didn't keep it very long. Because it soon learned how to escape its tether.

"Daddy!" our four-year-old son called to me one afternoon. "There's an animule in our yard!"

Racing out front, I found the Gallaghers' goat grazing under the shade of our large tulip poplar, which it seemed to prefer to its own sunny front yard. Its clothesline tether was strung out behind it, and it kept one eye on me as I approached. Then it began to dance about, kicking its heels, occasionally lowering its head as if to butt me. So I retreated to the house, telephoned Rich, and he abandoned his painting long enough to secure his goat.

The Gallaghers' goat got loose again the following day when Rich and Anne were out of town, coming over to graze beneath our tulip poplar. But I was able to catch it by the clothesline, drag it across the cul-de-sac, and retie it to the horseshoe stake. Soon after, however, it came right back to continue grazing, this time *without* its rope, having somehow learned to get the slip noose over its head. A few days later Rich put a dog collar around its neck, but that was no problem, ether. The goat simply chewed its way through the clothesline tether. So Rich yanked out the stake and gave up.

I don't know what he did with that goat.

I never asked.

Claude Clayton Smith

Pony Ride

They spent the afternoon
Riding the ponies.
Slowly clip-clopping
Along Rural Street
Around the corner
To the big pine woods.

Chatting and giggling
The way young girls do
With summer vacation
Stretched endlessly
Before them, with life,
And boys, on their minds.

They turned into the woods,
Dropping the reins then,
Letting the ponies
Meander at will
On thick pine needle
Carpets of forest floor.

Dust shimmered
Diamonds in sunlit shafts
Poking through green boughs.
Time stopped as they
Listened to the hum,
Cadence of the woods.

Much later they turned,
And saw only trees,
And sky ahead,
No exit behind,
Lazy leisure turned
To creeping panic.

Around in circles,
Up one path and down
Again, but the trees
All looked the same,
Giant, foreboding,
Dark and encroaching.

Twilight shadows splashed
Spooky pictures around.
Tiny woods creatures
Made like jungle
Monsters on the hunt
For little girls and ponies.

Then, not far away,
A car horn honked
Suddenly they knew
To the right, out of
The woods, back to
Rural Street and home.

Years later, decades,
No ponies this time,
No lazy summer ahead,
The boys gone, life lived.
Giant woods was still there,
It was . . . one block square.

Helen Carson

Bobcat

He came down through the green field
Like a wind-blown leaf will come.
We saw. The birds saw. They rose from
The brush, rattling like rain, reeled
Together through a short sky
And roosted. The cat didn't pause
But, loping, wasn't where he was.
Nothing there but my wife and I.
And when later a hawk rose
And fell on his winding stair,
He showed us the moving air
Between us and the bobcat's nose.

Laurence Snydal

Loneliness

The girl hunting with her father approaches
the strange man who has stopped at the end
of his day to rest and look at the lake.
Do you like geese? she asks. The man smiles.
The girl draws a webbed foot from her pocket
and places it in his hand. It's late fall,
and still the geese keep coming, two fingers
spread against a caution-yellow sky. Before
he can thank her, the girl has run off, down
to the edge of the water. The man studies her
father, about to bring down his third goose
today—then ponders the foot: soft, pink,
and covered with dirt like the little girl's hand.
He slides it into his coat pocket, and holds it there.

Meg Kearney

Carduelis Tristis

finches
Gold-   while
chime   flying
in   para-
swift   bolas.
Their
joy in
is the
making.

Rimas Uzgiris

Carolina Parakeet

On the walls of the courthouse are paintings
of winged creatures beautiful and desperate

as the people caged in the courtroom for the endless
trial. My mind is stripped bare

by the flock of witnesses passing through.
A pair of passenger pigeons with blue gray heads

and the mouth of one in the other's throat;
a wild turkey with exuberant russet plumes;

the Carolina parakeet with its crimson
and orange face, creamy bill,

feathers of viridescent green, a bird
extinct as hope. I wish for a way to end

this trial, before grief can
no longer be undone. At the end of the day

we gulp the sweet late afternoon air,
yawn with the trees. The swatch

of woods near the courthouse is ruffled green,
fragment of a once winged and glorious forest.

There on a branch deep in the dreamy leaves
I see an ivory prayer of a beak.

C. P. Mangel

Nest

It wasn't until we got the Christmas tree
into the house and up on the stand
that our daughter discovered a small bird's nest
tucked among its needled branches.

Amazing, that the nest had made it
all the way from Nova Scotia on a truck
mashed together with hundreds of other trees
without being dislodged or crushed.

And now it made the tree feel wilder,
a balsam fir growing in our living room,
as though at any moment a bird might flutter
through the house and return to the nest.

And yet, because we'd brought the tree indoors,
we'd turned the nest into the first ornament.
So we wound the tree with strings of lights,
draped it with strands of red beads,

and added the other ornaments, then dropped
two small brass bells into the nest, like eggs
containing music, and hung a painted goldfinch
from the branch above, as if to keep them warm.

Jeffrey Harrison

Practicing to Walk Like a Heron

My wife is at the computer. The cat
is sleeping across the soft gold cushion

of my chair. Last night there was a frost.
I am practicing to walk like a heron.

It's the walk of solemn monks
progressing to prayer on stilts,

the deliberate cadence of a waltz
in water. I lift my right leg within

the stillness, within the languid
quiet of a creek, slowly, slowly,

slowly set my foot on the dog-haired
carpet, pause, hold a half note, lift

the left, head steady as a bell before
the ringer tugs the rope. On I walk,

the heron's mute way, across the
room, past my wife who glances

up, holds her slender hands
above the keys until I pass.

Jack Ridl

Woman As Bird, Woman As Song

Elusive elegance of stature and gait:
the crown of her head drawn skyward,
shoulders spread like wings.

She is the song her chest is full of,
its rhythm is her stride:

Tall white heron balanced on an imaginary log
between earth which holds her down
and clouds that draw her skyward.

Sally Bliumis-Dunn

Zoological Crossroads

The sidra tree shook in the shamal. Nearby a wadi waited for winter rains. Sand-colored gerbils and girds zigzagged between desert squash and acacia. Lesser jerboas hibernated in their subterranean burrows a meter below ground. A Persian nightingale sang its fluty song among a throng of short-toed larks. A rear-fanged sand snake lazed lethargically beside the wadi as the desert gave no hint of Earth's potential for autumn. Dreams of a lusher locale whet my appetite like a mirage. But one succumbs to aridity and scarcity—learns to do without, remembers this is what the Desert Fathers were all about. One day, not a grain of sand stirring—stiflingly still. Next day, a shamal wind flinging a limb of the sidra against the window pane, shattering glass and shield from the searing sun. Dried-up wadi waiting, desert wheatear dozing in the acacia's shade. Winter would come again—the rains, wildflowers spreading across the barren waste with lavish fleeting grace, prying open Earth's unspeakable secrets. And I would understand what the searing sand says. But just then, alone, summer in the desert, I hoped for at least one stray camel, one oryx, one palm dove intoxicated on dates, one honey badger to lead me into the shade or a burrow under the sand to sleep through the day-long heat. All that desolation. And yet, where the biosphere's thin layer of complexity astounds. Across the sand, a false cobra left its dimpled pulse of an imprint. Heart of the desert, August's monochrome—nothing to write home about. Only at the edge, where expats and wealthy natives live with views of Gulf waters do bougainvillea, hibiscus and oleander thrive, fragile blossoms not hardy enough to survive without doting attention of faithful gardeners. But I would be the plain acacia or date palm living in the desert's heart—self-sufficiently strong.

Diana Woodcock

Jean Paucton, 69, Atop the Palais Garnier

In beekeepers' hood and canvas gauntlets,
he signals to follow him up an unsteady
ladder, out a narrow door, onto
a parapet two feet wide, a verdigris roof
sloping to nothing but sky on one side,
a skylight on the other—panes cracked
from previous visitors' panic.
Here, high above city mansards, steeples
and domes, Jean harvests honey
from his hives. Beside him, a huge
stone visage of Comedy laughs.
"It's my second career!—

I was a prop man here," he says, moving
through the dim backstage maze.
"*Cosi fan tutte,*" he remarks, pointing
to a bed used in the Mozart opera.
"Each year my bees give a thousand
pounds of honey I sell in the gift shop.
It tastes like flowers! My bees,"
he adds, thick black eyebrows rising
and falling, "fly to the chestnut trees
on the Champs-Elysees, the lindens
at the Palais Royal—even as far away
as the Bois de Boulogne!"

Wanda S. Praisner

The Alligator

The alligator is standing upright
outside my fourth floor window,
belly yellow and moist,
eyes blinking back afternoon sun.

He stands unmoving, tail balanced, ledge perched,
wind brushing the scales on his back.

I call the Fire Department
but they do not believe he is there.

Scientists say that a part of our brain
goes back to a reptilian past,
so perhaps my part has crawled out from my skull
and is whiling away the afternoon
in a form as vivid as flesh.

Near dusk he leaps and soars toward the sky,
dark eyes shining in red sunset wave,
as though they emit fire,
the same that warms our veins.

Lee Slonimsky

Pause

There are times I pause
at the bottom of the stairs
to note how well a chair fills a corner.

Mushrooms
spring from the empty lot next door
after a wet night

The sea replenishes the beach
with broken shells. Shapes, colors
tempt me to hold them
before they are ground to sand.

And most amazing: bones reknit
with only a forecaster's twinge to re-
member the fall. Flesh smoothes a raw sore.
In due season the eye regains its luster.

It's in the pause that I glimpse the healing.

Patti Tana

The Grid, the Net, and the Web

I recently overheard a woman say, "We live off the grid," a phrase I heard frequently twenty years ago, when people were trying to simplify their lives by growing or making more of what they really needed, while consuming less of whatever had to be bought, including electricity. "Living off the grid" meant that you created your own power rather than buying energy from a utility. Depending on what you could afford, you might use wood stoves or solar panels or hydropower or wind energy or geothermal wells or some combination. The idea was to make greater use of one's own resources, to demand less from the outside world, and to heed the words of our New England ancestors: "make over, make do, or do without."

I don't hear much about "living off the grid" these days, and even less about "doing without," especially doing without electricity. We live in interesting times. We can reduce our expenses and our carbon footprints by using energy-saving light bulbs, but we also have computers and are increasingly dependent upon the Internet. Some people actually seem addicted to the new style of communication. Connection must be instant, constant, and available everywhere. We talk or text or tweet or post or email day and night, and carry our phones with us so that this activity can go on uninterrupted, always.

When a friend jumps to answer a cell phone, or someone walks down the street with his head bent so low over a tiny screen that he can't see where he's going, I wonder where we're living now. Not "off the grid," that's for sure. Not "off" anything. We're always on: online, on the web, on call for family and friends and business associates. I think people are getting kind of jumpy from being "on" all the time, as if little alarms are buzzing at them all day long.

Do we ever take time off? Not just turning off the phone during a concert, or going offline for an hour only to come right back on again and check for messages. I'm talking about *off,* so that you feel the way someone does who has put up a sign on the door that says "Gone fishing," but doesn't say where or for how long.

I love communication. I'm a writer, for one thing, and there are people I love all over the world, for another. I work with a computer every day, thrilled that we've gone from dial-up to high-speed connection. I use a cell phone and email and Skype, and I'm tempted by Facebook and Twitter. Still, I think about "the grid" and "the net" and "the web." What's life like on a grid? Can't you get caught in a net? And isn't a web sometimes . . . well, sticky?

The technology is here to stay, though it will keep changing. It's very exciting, and really useful. But can we learn to relax with it, take it just a little easier? I hope so.

Reeve Lindbergh

Language by Immersion

Erica was supposed to be something of sensei.
I was struggling to learn sign language
And she was able to sign in over twelve languages

Including a few Plains Indian dialects.
But on our first lesson, when she brought me
To a scuba diving practice pool

I thought she was a charlatan.
She said underwater, my slowed gestures
Would become more precise,

Auditory distractions, a thing of the past.
She strapped on a tank and plugged an air hose in my mouth
Eliminating the possibility of lip reading.

And as we lowered ourselves into ten feet of water
She pointed at her mask with two fingers—
To keep my eyes on her.

As we touched bottom she began to sign
And asked me to respond in turn.
But I was having trouble concentrating no less.

So again, she motioned to keep my eyes on her.
This time she started to feel with her hands
For an imaginary wall and asked me to mimic her.

Then she pretended to pour herself
A glass of water—*pantomime!?*
Incensed, I bolted to the surface as she joined me,

I gave her something that amounted to
An Italian peace sign.
"That's great!" she said.

"Now, pretend I'm a motorist cutting you off.
Tell me the same thing in real sign."

Peter Moore

August Moonrise

Like a young woman
Averting her gaze
The pale pearl face
Of the moon rises
Over black pines—

Grows brighter, less
Coquettish in the
Indigo sky

Her lost twin trembles
On dark water

Jonathan Blake

The Stillness of Me

Walking the cliffs above the sea,
Looking for whales far out,
Wondering whether the sun would turn to rain,
I happened to look down and saw the earth move—
Tiny mounds of brown dirt shift
Ever so slightly upon the green lawn,
And then a tiny, pink nose, and tiny claws appeared.

Making sure not to block the sun,
I moved closer and closer,
Taking one small step and then another,
And each time the tiny face would disappear
For more of his movable feast.
Finally, I was close enough to see
Each tiny whisker on that cherubic face,
And while the sun turned to rain,
And perhaps a whale sailed by,
The tiny vole sniffed and sniffed
And looked about—
And never saw the stillness of me.

Kirk Gooding

Paper

What was written on me
were all the kinds of
silence. The silence of rocks
is not the same as the silence
of trees breathing.
What was written on us
were faint cries of owls,
the coyotes' siren yelps,
long threads of stars pulled through
night after night stitching
a script that said less
than a man might one morning
over coffee. Voles running
over the snow, now and then
a jet moving through each
of us—from our branch tips
to our roots binding the earth.
What was written on me
was the night watching
the night, without being called
night, or *stars,* or *tree,* or *snow.*
What was written on me
was written on everything.
It is still here.
What does it say?

Sam Taylor

When You're the Only Man in a Session on Women's Mysticism: 16th Century to Present

When you're the only man in a session on Women's Mysticism: 16th Century to Present, the first thing you have to think about is where you want to sit. There are six parabolic rows of maroon chairs spreading from the presentation table like sound waves from which to choose. Do you assert your patriarchal position front and center right away, or lurk in the insidious backroom margins, as though just keeping tabs on this session, making sure nothing gets too radical or out of control? You could sit right in the middle, but maybe that gives off the impression that you have no interest at all in women's mysticism, that you're there because you heard it would be a good place to mingle with and perhaps pick up women.

You're distressed by how judgmental you've imagined some of these scholars of women's mysticism to be. After all, you have a legitimate academic interest in Women's Mysticism: 16th Century to Present. You circled the session when you got your conference calendar and wrote an explanation point in the margin. You try to remember that they're not thinking about you, but focusing on the presenters and their work. They haven't even noticed you. Relax.

Then again, if you can be hypothetically disparaged for coming to a panel solely to pick up women, does that somehow mean there's something to it? Women's mysticism scholars *are* hot, and, yeah, maybe not the highest ratio of them are straight, but it's not like you have tons of competition either.

No. Remember, you are here to hear informative, scintillating papers. Sit down in the middle, take out a notebook and a pen, stare straight ahead and wait until someone starts reading.

It gets easier once it starts. The first three readers move you in all kinds of interesting places: from the Salem witch trials and Kristeva, to Margery Kempe and Jesus, to Willow and Tara in *Buffy*. You're taking notes. You're engaged.

Until the final reader, anyway, who starts reading every word of her paper like a poet turned loose from the Redwoods, taking the time to savor every single sound and syllable. That is to say, she is slow. You try to determine how long the piece will be by the stack of papers in front of her on the table. Not too high, but it is still going to take a while at this rate. But no, that is the wrong attitude. As some of the poets who read like that will remind you, a reading is a gift. Be generous in turn. Receive.

But you're reminded of the story of the child who was given one bicycle part every Christmas, finally having something close to a full bicycle when she turned 18. Where did you hear that story, anyway? Was it a church parable, Be grateful for every gift no matter how unexciting it seems at first? Or possibly an essay on the virtues of delayed gratification? Or was it an anecdote from someone's depressed childhood? After all, what is sadder than an 8-year-old carrying detached handlebars out to the dusty garage to wait with the other bicycle parts, discarded about like severed limbs amid empty gas cans and dusty cookbooks from the 1970s?

You remember where you are and notice that you're staring straight at the back of the neck of the person in front of you. You don't know how long the bicycle meditation was, how long you might have been fidgeting like a 15-year-old in church, neglecting the gift in front of you exactly like the bicycle parable might or might not have been warning against.

The reader is thanking people who helped her write her paper. She must be almost finished. It is time to redeem yourself. Showcase your interest, ask a question. Should you go witch trials, Kempe or *Buffy*? Better play it safe, stick with what you know: ask the *Buffy* presenter something about how magic-overdosed, black-eyed Willow fits into her notion of women's mysticism as a vehicle for lesbian representation in popular culture.

She looks at you, doesn't answer right away. She is probably just thinking about it. Sometimes it takes a while to respond—you know that. Still, she does seem to be taking quite a while. Did you miss an obvious point in her paper? You took notes and even wrote out the question— was the question offensive in some way? You're not sure. She is still looking at you and you look back. You wait.

Michael Palmer

Commentary

Sometime between the chaos of Genesis One
and the Tower of Babel in Eleven,
God created language with all its busy verbs,
its vowels and consonants,
its dark commandments.

The Patriarchs might say it started with Eve,
a kind of package deal, and point to the gossiping
of women. But it was Adam who named
the plants and animals, as if the fruit of a lemon
wouldn't prick the tongue without some arbitrary label.

I dream of the sounds of wind and water,
undifferentiated syllables of music.
And in the midst of all
these noisy books, this talk,
I grow intoxicated by silence.

Use your words, we tell our children now.
But without language, could the snake
have tempted Eve? And if you had
held your hand out wordless to me,
wouldn't I still have followed?

Linda Pastan

The Art of Waiting

The composer John Cage turned waiting into art. Musical art, that is. There's film footage of the distinguished-looking composer reminding us that if we're waiting for a train or a bus, for example, we should just listen. Noise can be music, he suggests, if we'll relax and enjoy it, listen for all the different tones, the repetitions, the rhythms, the surprises. Cage lived in Manhattan, so he knew all about noise.

I found Cage's lesson a hard one to accept, despite the great charm and obvious sincerity he displays in the interview. I was always an impatient sort of person, the sort who hates to be kept waiting and is often kept waiting because I'm impatient and arrive everywhere early! For me, waiting plus noise—airport noise, bus stop noise, rest-aurant noise, theater-before-the-performance noise—always equaled annoyance, period.

Somehow, though, images of Cage stayed with me as I began to reach the age where appreciation of life, life plain and simple, every moment of life, becomes a worthwhile pursuit. John Cage was white-haired in the interview I saw, and he looked like someone who had mastered that pursuit. I remember particularly how his long, gentle hands caressed the cat on his lap, how slow and easy his smile was. This was someone who was visibly alive, who enjoyed life. Cage's music is still considered difficult, even avant-garde, though he began to write music in the early 1930s. But there was nothing difficult about the man in the film.

Since I saw the documentary, I have tried hard to apply Cage's lessons. I love music, so surrounding myself with it is not so hard. In Cage's view, maybe I'm a composer! I've realized, too, that the lesson doesn't end with music. Other people may have a stronger connection to another of the arts. A visual person can make compositions from his whole field of vision, playing with perspective and scale and pattern and color. Then there's the great old standby of storytelling, imagining the lives of the people you see while you're waiting. No doubt Cage's long-time collaborator, choreographer Merce Cunningham, organized all he saw around him in terms of how people and animals and birds and vehicles and machines moved.

Then there are the scientist and mathematicians, artists in their own ways. How might they listen, and look, and organize all the sense impressions that surround us and impinge on us during the course of a half-hour wait in a public space? It's not hard to imagine becoming an expert at waiting, someone who can compose an epic, an opera, a film out of those moments just before the event we're waiting for. Maybe, too, when we finally get on the train, go into the office, wave to the arriving friend, we realize that we haven't been waiting at all, we've just been living through yet a few more of the events that make up the one great event we know as life.

Rebecca Taksel

Hope

Hope is what's left
at the end of the day—
after the floor's been swept,
the newspapers
are stacked,
after the long look
in the mirror
while brushing
my teeth before bed.

When I turn down
the covers of my grief,
I never cease
to be amazed
that hope is there
like a lost sock
I failed to discover
when I made the bed.

Julia Morris Paul

A Cup of Coffee

Suddenly I began to miss you.
Odd, it wasn't a memorable event like
a lost cat or a broken faucet.
It happened in just a moment,
I was turning out the light in the kitchen
suddenly you were there, in my mind.

I have craved these times alone.
Precious and too rare this isolation,
that allows thoughts to congeal uninterrupted
by conversation and need for connection.
Images that have lived in the outer rings of awareness
are able to combine into cohesive forms.

Time and interruption have become alarm clocks
waking me, reminding me of
what I must complete before the hour chimes.
Suddenly my fierce concentration
is broken by the memory of your voice.
"Hey, time for a cup of coffee."

Sara Hunsicker

Gratitude's Anniversary

One August afternoon, thirty-six years
(one for every measured yard) before,
when the company of my peers felt like
rows of folding chairs I had to walk between,
I took off my fringed moccasins, climbed
over the corral's split-post fence, and made
my way through Mt. Tremper's evergreens
to the stream below, whose song I followed
like the thread of conversation. Hurray
for pine needles, was the message sent up
from the soles, and there was the copse-hidden
brick oven where once we baked a pie from
wild berries. I wasn't allowed in the woods
alone; I was eleven. When I sat with my feet
in the water, just sat, ho, hum, a langoustine
darted out from a rock, like laughter, and I knew
I had come to a place of thrill and peacefulness,
heaven on earth. That day is related to this one.

Jessica Greenbaum

Contributors' Notes

Nin Andrews is the editor of a book of translations of the French poet Henri Michaux entitled *Someone Wants to Steal My Name*. She is also the author of several books including *The Book of Orgasms, Why They Grow Wings, Midlife Crisis with Dick and Jane, Sleeping with Houdini, Dear Professor, Do You Live in a Vacuum*, and *Southern Comfort*.

Jennifer Arin's poem "Ways We Hold," in this collection, is also the title poem of her book of verse (*Ways We Hold*, Dos Madres Press). Her poetry and essays have been published in both the U.S. and Europe, in *The AWP Writer's Chronicle*, and the *Paris/Atlantic Review*, among many others. Her awards include a grant from the National Endowment for the Humanities, a PEN Writer's Fund grant, and a Poets & Writers Writers-On-Site Residency.

Robin Behn is the author of five books of poems, most recently *Horizon Note* (University of Wisconsin Press), *Naked Writing* (Double Cross Press) and *The Yellow House* (Spuyten Duyvil Press). She teaches in the M.F.A in Creative Writing Program at The University of Alabama and for Vermont College of Fine Arts.

Lorna Knowles Blake's first collection of poems, *Permanent Address*, won the Richard Snyder Memorial Prize from the Ashland Poetry Press. Poems have appeared recently or are forthcoming in *The Hudson Review* and *Literary Imagination*, among others. She has been the recipient of a residency from the Virginia Center for the Creative Arts and a Walter E. Dakin Fellowship from the Sewanee Writers Conference.

Jonathan Blake lives and writes in Fitchburg, Ma. Currently he is a member of the English department at Worcester

State University. Recent poems have appeared in *Poetry East, Shadow and Light – A Literary Anthology on Memory*, and *Amoskeag*. His essay *King of the Wood* can be found in the *Worcester Review* commemorating Stanley Kunitz' one-hundredth birthday.

Sally Bliumis-Dunn teaches Modern Poetry and Creative Writing at Manhattanville College. In 2002, she was a finalist for the Nimrod/Hardman Pablo Neruda Prize. Her poems have been published in *The Paris Review, Prairie Schooner, Poetry* London, and the NYT, among others. Her first book, *Talking Underwater*, was published in 2007 and her second book, *Second Skin*, was published in 2010, both by Wind Publications.

Mark Brazaitis is the author of four books of fiction, including *The Incurables: Stories*, winner of the 2012 Richard Sullivan Prize from the University of Notre Dame Press. His book of poems, *The Other Language*, won the 2008 ABZ Poetry Prize. He is an associate professor of English and directs the Creative Writing Program at West Virginia University.

Daniel Brown's poems have appeared in *Poetry, Partisan Review, Parnassus: Poetry in Review, The New Criterion* and other journals. Winner of a Pushcart Prize, Brown has been widely anthologized in volumes such as *Poetry 180*, edited by Billy Collins, and *Fathers*, edited by David Ray. His *Why Bach?*, an appreciation of Bach's music, is available on the Internet.

Melissa Carl is a multiple Pushcart nominee. She has published in a variety of e-zines, magazines, journals, anthologies, and other publications including *cellpoems*, the *In Posse Review, CircleShow, Off the Coast Magazine*, and *Amoskeag: The Journal of Southern New Hampshire University*. She gives regular readings in the Central PA and Maryland, where she also teaches.

Helen Carson is the author of "Pony Ride" in this anthology. Unfortunately, we do not have information about her.

Joanne Chin is a graduate of the Rutgers-Newark MFA Program. She has worked as a research assistant at the Dana-Farber Cancer Institute, in Boston. Currently, she is working on a collection of short stories, tentatively titled *Light the House.*

Barbara Crooker's poems have appeared in magazines such as *The Green Mountains Review, The Denver Quarterly,* and anthologized in *Good Poems for Hard Times* and *Good Poems American Places* (Garrison Keillor, editor) (Viking Penguin) and the *Bedford Introduction to Literature.* Her newest book is *More* (C&R Press, 2010).

Steve Cushman has published two novels, *Heart With Joy* and *Portis-ville,* as well as the short story collection *Fracture City.* For the past twenty years, Steve has worked as an X-ray Technologist and currently works at Moses Cone Memorial Hospital in Greensboro, North Carolina.

Todd Davis teaches creative writing and environmental studies at Penn State University's Altoona College. He is the author of four books of poems, most recently *In the Kingdom of the Ditch* and *The Least of These,* both from Michigan State University Press. His poetry has been nominated for the Pushcart Prize, has won the Gwendolyn Brooks Poetry Prize.

Shira Dentz is the author of *black seeds on a white dish* (Shearsman Books), a book of poems that was nominated for the PEN/Osterweil Award 2011. She is also the author of a chapbook, *Leaf Weather* (Tilt Press), and *door of thin skin*s, a forthcoming book from CavanKerry Press.

Sally Lipton Derringer's book manuscript was a finalist for Fordham University's Poets Out Loud Prize and the New Issues Poetry Prize. Her poems have appeared in *Poet Lore,*

The Los Angeles Review, Bellevue Literary Review, and other journals and anthologies. She has an M.A. in Creative Writing from Antioch University and currently teaches at Rockland Center for the Arts in West Nyack, N.Y.

Moyra Donaldson is a poet and creative writing facilitator who lives and works in Co Down, Northern Ireland. She has four collections of poetry, the most recent, *Miracle Fruit* was published in 2010 from Lagan Press, Belfast. Her *Selected Poems* is forthcoming from Liberties Press, Dublin in July 2012 .

Marta Ferguson's chapbook *Mustang Sally Pays Her Debt to Wilson Pickett* was published by Main Street Rag in 2005. Recent work has appeared in *Spillway, Bluestem,* and as a finalist in *Alligator Juniper* 2012 contest issue. Marta is the sole proprietor of Wordhound Writing & Editing Services, LLC.

Kathleen Gerard writes across genres. She is the author of *In Transit,* a novel which was awarded Best Romantic Fiction at The New York Book Festival 2011. Gerard's short fiction has been awarded The Perillo Prize, The Eric Hoffer Prose Award and was nominated for Best New American Voices.

Bernadette Geyer is the author of the poetry chapbook, *What Remains* (Argonne House Press), and recipient of a 2010 Strauss Fellowship from the Arts Council of Fairfax County. Her poems have appeared in *Oxford American, North American Review, Verse Daily, The Midwest Quarterly,* and elsewhere. Geyer works as a freelance writer and copy editor in the Washington, DC, area.

Maria Mazziotti Gillan is a recipient of the 2011 Barnes & Noble Writers for Writers Award from Poets & Writers, and the 2008 American Book Award for her book, *All That Lies Between Us* (Guernica Editions). Her latest book is *What*

We Pass On: Collected Poems 1980-2009 (Guernica Editions, 2010), and she has a book forthcoming in September 2012, *The Place I Call Home* (New York Quarterly Books).

Matthew Kirk Gooding is a family doctor who has published poems in The Journal Of The American Medical Association. Recently he collected his poems under hard cover. He began painting with acrylics at the age of 64 and there is always a canvas on his easel. He lives with his wife, Shannon Rio, Nurse Practitioner, in Ashland, Oregon.

Jessica Greenbaum's first book, *Inventing Difficulty,* came out from The Gerald Cable Prize. "Gratitude's Anniversary" appears in her second book, *The Two Yvonne's,* which appeared in fall 2012 as the selection for Princeton University Press' Series of Contemporary Poetry. She is the poetry editor of *upstreet,* and is grateful, also, to be hanging with the readers in the waiting room

Jeffrey Harrison is the author of four full-length books of poems—most recently *Incomplete Knowledge* (Four Way Books), which was runner-up for the Poets' Prize in 2008—as well as of *The Names of Things* (2006), a selection published by the Waywiser Press in the U.K. He is the recipient of Guggenheim and NEA Fellowships.

Dolores Hayden's poems have appeared in many journals and anthologies including *The Yale Review, Southwest Review, Raritan,* and *Best American Poetry 2009.* She's published two poetry collections, *American Yard* (2004) and *Nymph, Dun, and Spinner* (2010), and received awards from the Poetry Society of America, the New England Poetry Club, the Virginia Center for Creative Arts, and the Djerassi Foundation. She teaches at Yale University.

Roxanne Hoffman worked on Wall Street, and now answers a patient hotline for a New York home healthcare provider. Her work has been published in literary journals like *Amaze: The Cinquain Journal*, and *Clockwise Cat*, and in several anthologies including *The Bandana Republic:* (Soft Skull Press) and *Love after 70* (Wising Up Press). "In Loving Memory," a chapbook, was released December 2011.

Sara Hunsicker was born and raised in the mid-west. A retired speech/language pathologist, she now lives in New Jersey. Sara learned to love the process of writing while being treated for cancer. She participates in writing and poetry groups and attends classes at a local university.

Frank Huyler is an emergency physician in Albuquerque, New Mexico. He is also the author of the essay collection *The Blood of Strangers* as well as the novels *Right of Thirst* and *The Laws of Invisible Things*. His poetry has appeared in *The Atlantic Monthly*, *The Georgia Review*, and *Poetry*, among others.

Susan Jackson's poetry collection *Through a Gate of Trees* was published by CavanKerry Press in 2007. In addition to her prose pieces, Susan's poems have appeared in the recent issue of *Tiferet, A Journal of Spiritual Literature, When the Muse Calls: Poems For The Creative Life edited by Kathryn Ridall,* and the Delaware Art Museum's *Painted Poetry: The Art of Mary Page Evans.*

Meg Kearney's newest collection of poems, *Home By Now*, won the 2010 PEN New England LL Winship Award and was a finalist for the Paterson Poetry Prize and Foreword Magazine Book of the Year. She is also author of two novels-in-verse for teens: *The Secret of Me* (Persea 2005) and its sequel, *The Girl in the Mirror* (2012). Meg directs the Solstice MFA in Creative Writing Program of Pine Manor College in Massachusetts.

Elizabeth Kim is a native of Philadelphia where she received her BA in English from Temple University and was awarded the William Van Wert Award. She is currently a student at the MFA program at Rutgers-Newark.

Maxine Kumin is a former US Poet Laureate and winner of the Pulitzer and Ruth Lilly prizes. She is the author of *Where I Live: New & Selected Poems 1990-2010* (Norton), her 17th volume, which won the 2011 L.A. Times poetry book prize. She has taught at numerous places and served on the Bread Loaf Writers Conference faculty for seven years.

Quincy R. Lehr is the author of two collections of poetry, *Across the Grid of Streets* and *Obscure Classics of English Progressive Rock*. His poetry and criticism have appeared in numerous journals in North America, Europe, and Australia, and he is the associate editor of *The Raintown Review*. He lives in Brooklyn, where he teaches history.

Phillis Levin is the author of four volumes of poetry, most recently *Mercury* (Penguin, 2001) and *May Day* (Penguin, 2008), and is the editor of *The Penguin Book of the Sonnet* (2001). Her honors include a Fulbright Scholar Award to Slovenia, the Amy Lowell Poetry Travelling Scholarship, and fellowships from the Guggenheim Foundation and the National Endowment for the Arts.

Janice Levy is the author of 20 children's books. Her adult fiction appears in numerous anthologies and literary magazines. She teaches writing at Hofstra University.

Reeve Lindbergh is the author of more than two dozen books for children and adults. Her work has also appeared in the *New York Times Book Review*, *The New Yorker* and *The Washington Post*. She lives in Barnet, Vermont, with her husband, writer Nat Tripp, and an assortment of animals, enjoying visits from their children and grandchildren.

C.P Mangel was corporate counsel for over twenty years, and is completing a Master of Fine Arts in Creative Writing through the University of British Columbia. She lives in North Carolina with her husband, four children and three rescue mixed-breed muses.

Janet McCann is an old Texas poet who has been teaching Creative Writing at Texas A&M University since 1969. Most recent collections are *Emily's Dress* (Pecan Grove Press) and *House* (Plan B Press.)

Gardner McFall is the author of two books of poems, *The Pilot's Daughter* and *Russian Tortoise*, as well as two children's books, and an opera libretto called, *Amelia*, commissioned and premiered by Seattle Opera. Her work has appeared in *The Atlantic Monthly, Southwest Review, Sewanee Review, Tin House, Paris Review,* and elsewhere. She lives in New York City.

Britt Melewski (poetry) grew up in New Jersey and Puerto Rico. His poems have appeared in *Off the Coast, Liebamour, the DMQ Review* and other journals. He lives in Brooklyn.

Peter Moore studied in the *Classes Préparatoires aux Grandes Écoles Vétérinaires* in Paris. His work has previously appeared in *The Raritan Review, The Massachusetts Review* and *Hotel Amerika,* among other journals.

Rena J. Mosteirin is a Cuban-American author of fiction and poetry. Her poetic novella *Nick Trail's Thumb* was selected by Lydia Davis and published by Kore Press in 2008. She is a native New Yorker and a graduate of Dartmouth College.

Paula Neves has an MFA in poetry from the MFA in Writing Program at Rutgers-Newark, teaches English composition, and is always wondering where to travel to next. Her poetry, fiction and non-fiction have appeared in various publications.

Martha (Patty) Oliver-Smith lives in northern Vermont and has been a teacher of high school and college writing and literature courses for many years. She began writing poetry about twenty years ago at the suggestion of a physician/poet friend. Currently, she is working on a full-length memoir about three generations of women artists in her family.

Michael Palmer lives in Lubbock, Texas where he is completing his PhD in English. His work has appeared in the *Georgetown Review, Sunstone, Wag's Revue,* and other magazines.

Linda Pastan's thirteenth book of poems, *Traveling Light,* has recently been published by Norton. She was Poet Laureate of Maryland from 1991-1995 and has been a finalist twice for the National Book Award. In 2003 she won the Ruth Lilly Poetry Prize.

Julia Morris Paul's poems have been published or are forthcoming in such journals as *Connecticut Review, New Mexico Review, Common Ground Review,* and in anthologies, including *Lavandaria, an Anthology of Women, Wash and Word* and *Water's Edge: Open to Interpretation.* She was a 2010 finalist for the May Swenson Poetry Prize and the Blue Lynx Prize. She serves on the boards of the Connecticut Poetry Society and Riverwood Poetry Series.

Molly Peacock has published six volumes of poetry, most recently *The Second Blush* from W.W. Norton and Company. Her poems are widely anthologized in the *Oxford Book of American Poetry* and *The Best of the Best American Poetry.* She is also the author of *The Paper Garden: An Artist Begins Her Life's Work at 72.*

Tamra Plotnick has published poems, stories, essays and translations in journals and anthologies including *Tribes #8* and *Global City Review.* She has penned a novel, set in Brazil, the Caribbean and The East Village of New York City. A former editor of *Promethean,* she holds two Master's degrees and currently teaches English to public high school students in the heart of Brooklyn.

Dawn Potter is the author of three collections of poetry, most recently *How the Crimes Happened* (CavanKerry Press, 2010). Her memoir, *Tracing Paradise: Two Years in Harmony with John Milton* (University of Massachusetts Press, 2009), won the 2010 Maine Literary Award in Nonfiction. Currently she is associate director of the Frost Place Conference on Poetry and Teaching.

Wanda S. Praisner, a recipient of fellowships from the NJ State Council on the Arts and the Geraldine R. Dodge Foundation, is author of *A Fine and Bitter Snow* (Palanquin P), *On the Bittersweet Avenues of Pomona* (winner of the Spire Press Poetry Chapbook Competition, 2005), and *Where the Dead Are,* forthcoming from CavanKerry Press. She is a resident poet for the State Council on the Arts.

Kristin Prevallet's writings on poetics and consciousness have appeared in a variety of publications. She is the author of four books including *I, Afterlife: Essay in Mourning Time* (Essay Press, 2007) and *Shadow, Evidence, Intelligence* (Factory School, 2006). In March 2012, The Belladonna Collaborative will publish her most recent book, *Everywhere Here and in Brooklyn: A Four Quartets.*

Susanna Rich is an Emmy Award nominee, Fulbright Fellow in Creative Writing, and author of two Finishing Line Press chapbooks: *Television Daddy* and *The Drive Home.* She founded Wild Nights Productions, LLC. Susanna is Professor of English at Kean University and was awarded the Presidential Excellence Award for Distinguished Teaching.

Jack Ridl's *Broken Symmetry* (Wayne State University Press) was co-recipient of The Society of Midland Authors best book of poetry award for 2006. His collection *Losing Season* (CavanKerry Press) was named the best sports book of the year for 2009 by The Institute for International Sport. His collection *Practicing to Walk Like a Heron* will be published in 2013 (Wayne State University Press.)

Benjamin K. Rogers has been a life long resident of Louis-
iana and attended college in Dallas, Texas, where he studied
playwriting. He returned to Louisiana and persued poetry
crafting at LA Tech. His five books of poetry, *Holding Five
Aces, Returning from the Pyramid, Small Potatoes, The Glory
Gauntlet,* and *Light Vs. Stone,* may be read through his web-
site, BenjaminKRogers.com.

Liz Rosenberg is the award-winning author of 4 books of po-
ems and two novels, as well as numerous children's books. Her
newest novel, *The Laws of Gravity,* will be out from the new
Amazon Publishing in March of 2012. She teaches English
and Creative writing at the State U of NY at Binghamton
and writes a book column for the Boston Globe.

Natania Rosenfeld is Professor of English at Knox College in
Galesburg, Illinois, and the author of Outsiders Together:
Virginia and Leonard Woolf (Princeton University Press,
2000). Her poems, essays and stories have appeared in nu-
merous journals.

Roberto F. Santiago received the BA from Sarah Lawrence
College and the MFA from Rutgers University. His po-
etry has been published in such anthologies as *Collective
Brightness* (Sibling Rivalry Press) (2011), *Me No Habla
With Acento El Museo* (Rebel Satori Press) (2011), among
others. Roberto has also been awarded the 2011 Alfred C.
Carey Prize for Spoken Word Poetry.

Martha Serpas's two poetry collections are *Côte Blanche* and
The Dirty Side of the Storm. Her work has appeared in *The New
Yorker* and *The Nation,* and in anthologies such as *The Art
of the Sonnet* and *American Religious Poems. Veins in the Gulf,*
a documentary, features her poetry. She teaches at the
University of Houston and is a hospital trauma chaplain.

Myra Shapiro is the author of two books of poems *I'LL
See You Thursday* (Blue Sofa Press, 1996) *and Loneliness*

and Plenty (Antrim House Books, 2012) and a memoir, *Four Sublets: Becoming a Poet in New York* (Chicory Blue Press, 2007). She is a former high school English teacher and a teacher of poetry workshops.

Lee Slonimsky has published four books of poems, *Talk Between Leaf and Skin, Pythagoras in Love, Money and Light*, and most recently, *Logician of the Wind*. He has been nominated for the Pushcart Prize six times. Lee is also the co-author of the Lee Carroll novels, *Black Swan Rising, The Watchtower,* and *The Shape Stealer*, along with his wife, Hammett Award winning mystery writer Carol Goodman.

Claude Clayton Smith is the author of a novel, two children's books, and four books of creative nonfiction. He is also co-editor/translator of *The Way of Kinship*, an anthology of Native Siberian literature. His latest book is *Ohio Outback: Learning to Love the Great Black Swamp* (Kent State University Press, 2010). He is Professor Emeritus of English at Ohio Northern University.

Michael Snediker is a professor of American Literature and Poetics at Queen's University, Kingston Ontario. His poems have appeared in journals including *Black Warrior Review, Crazyhorse, Court Green, Jubilat,* and *The Paris Review*. He has published two poetry chapbooks, *Nervous Pastoral* (doveltail books) and *Bourdon* (White Rabbit Press).

Laurence Snydal is a poet, musician and retired teacher. He has published more than 100 poems in such magazines as *Columbia, Caperock, Lyric* and *Gulf Stream* and in many anthologies including *The Years Best Fantasy and Horror,* and *Visiting Frost*. Some of his work has been performed in New York City and Baltimore.

Elizabeth Spires is the author of six collections of poetry, including *Worldling, Now The Green Grass Balde Rises,* and *The Wave-Maker.* She has also written six books for young readers, including *The Mouse of Amherst,* the tale of a white mouse who lives in Emily Dickinson's room. Her poems have appeared in *The New Yorker, The Atlantic, Poetry,* and many other magazines. She lives in Baltimore and teaches at Goucher College.

Ellen Steinbaum is the author of two poetry collections, *After-words* and *Container Gardening.* Her work has been nominated for a Pushcart Prize and included in Garrison Keillor's new anthology, *Good Poems, American Places.* She is the author of a one-person play CenterPiece. She is a former literary columnist for The Boston Globe and now writes a blog.

Rebecca Taksel is a contributing editor of the *Redwood Coast Review,* a literary magazine published in Mendocino County, California. She lives in Pittsburgh, Pennsylvania, where she teaches French and English at Point Park University. She is never late, always punctual, often early, and so has spent many, many hours waiting.

Patti Tana is Professor Emerita of English at Nassau Community College (SUNY) and the author of eight collections of poems, most recently *Any Given Day* (Whittier Publications, Inc., 2011). The Walt Whitman Birthplace Association selected her as their Long Island Poet of the Year 2009. She is the editor of the *Songs of Seasoned Women* poetry anthology and associate editor of the *Long Island Quarterly.*

Adam Tavel received the 2010 Robert Frost Award, and his first poetry collection, *The Fawn Abyss,* is forthcoming from Salmon Poetry in 2014. Tavel is the poetry editor for *Conte* and an associate professor of English at Wor-Wic Community College on Maryland's Eastern Shore.

Sam Taylor is the author of *Body of the World,* a collection of poems that explore themes of mysticism and mortality in a variety of contemporary contexts. It is available from Copper Canyon Press. Born and raised in Miami, he has lived in California, New Mexico, Texas, and Virginia, and he currently teaches at Wichita State University in Wichita, Kansas.

Maria Terrone is the author of two poetry collections: *A Secret Room in Fall*, co-winner of the McGovern Prize from Ashland Poetry Press, and *The Bodies We Were Loaned*, plus a chapbook, *American Gothic, Take 2*. Her poems have appeared in such magazines as *The Hudson Review, Poetry,* and *Ploughshares* and in 20 anthologies.

Vincent J. Tomeo has been published in the New York Times, Comstock Review, Mid-America Poetry Review, among others. He has 617 published poems and have won a total of 81 awards.

Vincent Toro is a Puerto Rican poet, playwright, director, and educator. He is a finalist for the Allen Ginsberg poetry prize and winner of the Metlife Nuestras Voces playwriting award. His work has been published magazines including *Vallum* (2007), *Bordersenses* (2007), and the *San Antonio Express News Poetry Page* (3/2011). His work is also forthcoming in the anthology CHORUS, edited by Saul Williams (2012).

Rimas Uzgiris' poetry and translations have been published in numerous magazines and is forthcoming in *Quiddity, Atlanta Review, Hudson Review,* among others. His book reviews have been published or are forthcoming in *HTML Giant, Rumpus* and *Post Road*. He holds a Ph.D. in philosophy from the University of Wisconsin-Madison, and received an MFA in creative writing from Rutgers-Newark University.

Rosanna Warren, the author of four collections of poetry, has received awards from the Academy of Arts and Letters and has won the Lamont Poetry Prize. She teaches at Boston University and lives in Jamaica Plain, Massachusetts.

Richard Marx Weinraub was born in New York City in 1949 and is related to the Marx Brothers through his mother. A book of his poetry entitled *Wonder Bread Hill* was published in 2002 by the University of Puerto Rico Press. His poetry has appeared in many journals including *The Paris Review* and the *Asheville Poetry Review*. In 2012, Poets Wear Prada will publish his full-length book of poetry entitled *Lapidary*.

Diana Woodcock is the author of *Swaying on the Elephant's Shoulders*, which won the 2010 Vernice Quebodeaux International Poetry Prize for Women (Little Red Tree Publishing, 2011). Her three chapbooks include *In the Shade of the Sidra Tree*, a nominee for the National Book Critics Circle Award (Finishing Line Press), *Mandala* (Foothills Publishing), and *Travels of a Gwai Lo*—the title poem of which was nominated for a Pushcart Prize.

Acknowledgments

Sincere thanks to the editors of the publications in which these poem and prose pieces, some in different versions, first appeared.

"So Large" by Daniel Brown appeared in *The New Criterion* (under the title "A Giant") and in *Taking the Occasion* (Dee, 2008).

"As If There Were Only One" by Martha Serpas first appeared in *Côte Blanche* (2002).

"Celerity" by Shira Dentz first appeared in *black seeds on a white dish* by Shira Dentz (Shearsman, 2010).

"Our Old Pond" by Maxine Kumin first appeared in *New Hampshire Home Magazine* (July/August 2010).

"'In Heaven It Is Always Autumn,'" from *Now The Green Blade Rises: Poems* by Elizabeth Spires. Copyright © 2002 by Elizabeth Spires. Used by permission of W. W. Norton & Company, Inc.

"Acorn," from *May Day* by Phillis Levin, copyright © 2008 by Phillis Marna Levin. Used by permission of Penguin, a division of Penguin Group (USA), Inc.

"Ice Storm" by Quincy Lehr first appeared in the U.K. journal *New Walk 1* (autumn 2010).

"Bloodstone" by Richard Marx Weinraub first appeared in book of poetry entitled *Lapidary* by Richard Marx Weinraub, published in 2012 by Poets Wear Prada.

"Windowless" by Kristin Prevallet first appeared in *Barrow Street* (2003).

"Lightning Strike" by Moyra Donaldson appeared in *The Horses' Nest* (Belfast: Lagan, 2006).

"Ways We Hold" by Jennifer Arin appeared in *Ways We Hold* by Jennifer Arin (Dos Madres, 2012).

"Three Horses" by Robin Behn is from *When She Named Fire: An Anthology of Contemporary Poetry by American Women*, ed. Andrea Hollander Budy (Autumn House, 2008).

"After a Fairy Tale by Oscar Wilde" is from *The Pilot's Daughter* by Gardner McFall. Copyright © 1996 by Time Being Books. Re-printed by permission of Time Being Press.

"Eclogue 2" is from *How the Crimes Happened* by Dawn Potter, reprinted by permission of CavanKerry Press, Ltd.

"The Art of Giving" by Kathleen Gerard appeared in *Feile-Festa* (spring 2009) and *Bigger Than They Appear: Anthology of Very Short Poems* (Accents, 2011).

"Southern Comfort" is from *Southern Comfort* by Nin Andrews, reprinted by permission of CavanKerry Press, Ltd. It also appeared in *Sentence 4* (2006) and *The Alhambra Calendar 2008.*

"Bliss" by Todd Davis first appeared in the *Journal of Kentucky Studies* (2010).

"Beets" by Maria Terrone first appeared in *Blueline* (1999).

"Ode to Chocolate" by Barbara Crooker first appeared in *The MacGuffin* and then in *More* by Barbara Crooker (C&R Press, 2010).

"The Inheritance" by Myra Shapiro appeared in *I'll See You Thursday* by Myra Shapiro (Ally Press, 1996) and in *Calyx* 17, no. 1 (1997).

"standing at the shore" by Ellen Steinbaum appeared in *Container Gardening*, published by CW Books in 2008, Cincinnati, Ohio.

"Breaktide" by Michael Snediker first appeared in the chapbook *Nervous Pastoral*, published in 2008 by doveltail books.

"Walking Holly down a Wooded Lane" by Susanna Rich first appeared in *POEM {Huntsville Literary Association} 96* (November 2006).

"My Dog Grandma" by Vincent J. Tomeo first appeared in *Poets' Podium* (Ontario, Calif.: Spring, 2007).

"Loneliness" by Meg Kearney was originally published in *An Unkindness of Ravens* (BOA Editions, 2001).

"Nest" by Jeffrey Harrison first appeared in *upstreet* (summer 2012).

"Practicing to Walk Like a Heron" by Jack Ridl first appeared in the *Colorado Review* (spring 2010).

"Woman As Bird, Woman As Song" by Sally Bliumis-Dunn was published in *Talking Underwater* (Wind, 2007).

"Pause" by Patti Tana was first published in *Ask the Dreamer Where Night Begins: Poems & Postscripts* by Patti Tana (Kendall/ Hunt, 1986) and was included in *Make Your Way Across This Bridge: New & Selected Writings* by Patti Tana (Whittier, 2003). "Pause" is reprinted with permission of the author.

"The Grid, the Net, and the Web" by Reeve Lindbergh was a commentary written by Reeve Lindbergh for Vermont Public Radio and aired on May 4, 2011.

"Language by Immersion" by Peter Moore was originally published in *Gargoyle* 55 (2009).

"Paper" by Sam Taylor first appeared in *Meridian 18* (January 2007).

"Commentary" by Linda Pastan first appeared in the winter 2011 issue of *CCAR Journal: The Reform Jewish Quarterly*.

"Hope" by Julia Morris Paul first appeared in *Caduceus 6* (2008).

"Gratitude's Anniversary" by Jessica Greenbaum appeared in *The Two Yvonnes*, published by Princeton University Press (2012).

Books by Rachel Hadas

The Golden Road, 2012
Strange Relation, 2011
The Ache of Appetite, 2010
Classics, 2007
Three Poets in Conversation, 2007
River of Forgetfulness, 2006
Laws (200 Press), 2004 (Poetry)
Indelible, 2001
Merrill, Cavafy, Poems, and Dreams, 2001
Halfway Down the Hall, 1998
The Double Legacy, 1995
The Empty Bed, 1995
Other Worlds Than This, 1994
Mirrors of Astonishment, 1992
Living in Time, 1990
Pass It On, 1989
A Son from Sleep, 1987
Form, Cycle, Infinity: Landscape Imagery in the Poetry of Robert Frost & George Seferis, 1985
Slow Transparency, 1983
Starting from Troy, 1975

Books Edited by Rachel Hadas

The Greek Poets, 2009 (ed. with Peter Constantine,
Edmumd Keeley, and Karen Van Dyck)
Unending Dialogue: Voices from an AIDS Poetry Workshop, 1993
(ed. with Charles Barber)

Other Books in the LaurelBooks Series

CavanKerry's Mission

CavanKerry Press is a not-for-profit literary press
dedicated to art and community. From its inception in
2000, its vision has been to present, through poetry and
prose, *Lives Brought to Life* and to create programs that
bring CavanKerry books and writers to diverse audiences.

Ordering Information:

The Waiting Room Reader II: Words to Keep You Company is available for purchase wherever books are sold.

If you would like to order copies of
The Waiting Room Reader II: Words to Keep You Company
for your medical facility, please contact:
Donna Rutkowski: *The Waiting Room Reader II* Administrator
at donna@cavankerrypress.org

www. cavankerrypress.org
www.humanism-in-medicine.org